THE FOUR SEASONS WHOLEFOOD COOKBOOK

Elegant vegetarian recipes and enticing festive menus to provide nutritional balance and variety all year round.

THE FOUR SEASONS WHOLEFOOD COOKBOOK

Nutritionally balanced recipes making the best use of seasonally available foods

by

Susan Thorpe

N.D., D.O., M.B.N.O.A.

Illustrated by Paul Turner

THORSONS PUBLISHERS INC.
New York

Thorsons Publishers Inc.
Distributed to the trade by
Inner Traditions International Ltd.,
377 Park Avenue South
New York, New York 10016

First published 1983

British Library Cataloguing in Publication Data

Thorpe, Susan
    The four seasons wholefood cookbook
    1. Vegetarian cookery
    I. Title
    641.5′636   TX837

    ISBN 0-7225-0748-8

Printed in Hong Kong by South China Printing Co.

Contents

Acknowledgements

My thanks to Noela Simpson for starting me on this path; John and Simon for their good humour; Joan Lay for her guidance and encouragement; Yvonne Hatfield for her inspiration with beans and lentils; Doris Grant for permission to use her famous 'Daily Bread' recipe; Joy Bennet for her organization of the lay-out and her untiring and unerring typing.

Foreword

Susan Thorpe is to be congratulated on producing such an original and creative wholefood cookbook. In its comprehensive outlook it fulfils a real need among a readership increasingly interested in health and food. The emphasis is on preparing our meals in closer harmony with the offerings of the seasons. This brings us closer to the laws of nature which should result in increased health and wellbeing. The book reveals a dedicated, scientifically well-informed and imaginative cook who deeply cares about both delicious and health-giving food.

The introduction gives sound guidelines on the important art of making the best use of nature's gifts to us, her all too often careless and deviant children. The interesting menu suggestions have the added advantage of being suitable for slimmers and provide 'an elegant sufficiency', enhanced by unexpected spices, and natural flavourings. The emphasis is on quality nutrition rather than quantity. Here we do well to remember that according to the great Scottish physician Dr Abernethy, 'One third of what we eat keeps us alive, the other two thirds keep the doctor alive!' — and who wants that?

Giving Imperial, metric and American measures for every recipe is both useful and a training in adaptability. The seasonal colour plates are delightfully instructive and so are the line drawings.

Susan Thorpe's lack of fanaticism about certain ingredients frowned upon by purists, I find particularly endearing. It will appeal to those who are reluctant about giving up conventional foods, and hopefully win more adherents for food that is more health-promoting, ecologically sound, and more compassionate in relation to animals and the Third World at the same time.

I congratulate the author on her excellent book and hope that readers will enjoy using it as much as I (a critical vegetarian wholefood cook of fifty years experience) have enjoyed reading it.

BARBARA LATTO M.D.

FOR JUDY, MY SISTER

Introduction

People who come to see me at my osteopathic practice in Kent often ask for recipes to help them change from an indifferent to a health-promoting diet, and I am also asked by would-be vegetarians for guidance in changing over from meat.

It is largely this that prompted me to write this book, although I began thinking up the recipes in it about ten years ago when my family and I decided to take better care of ourselves. There is no doubt at all that the most healthy and simple way to eat is the natural way, choosing as the basis of the diet those foods that are freshest and in greatest variety at any particular time of the year. This way one is in sympathy with the natural rhythm of the seasons. (A few of the recipes in this book make use of ingredients which are readily available all year round. These are economical and nutritious dishes to prepare at any time of the year.)

As a general rule, the aim is to combine the essential foods so that meals consist of 40-60 per cent fruit and vegetables, 20-25 per cent protein foods, 15-20 per cent carbohydrate foods and about 10 per cent polyunsaturated fats. The percentages are variable to allow for different individual needs.

The way to eat well is to eat food as close as possible to its natural form. Nature produces easily digestible, complementary combinations of nutrients, and always provides enough fibre to ensure they will all pass through the digestive system efficiently. Nature also provides salt in food, and the use of too much additional salt in cooking can be harmful to health and tends to mask the delicate flavours of the ingredients.

Select your cooking utensils very carefully. Heavy stainless steel saucepans are a pleasure to use and to clean, and they are safe, but they are also expensive. Good quality enamel is fine, but rather prone to chipping if knocked, and *Pyrex* glass, whilst probably the best for your health, is also fragile. Avoid aluminium and coated saucepans.

Always use lids to preserve flavour and nutrients, and cook as little as possible. Food value decreases with high temperatures and over-cooking. Greens such as spinach, kale and broccoli cook very well with the addition of a knob of butter and the juice of half a lemon and very little water. Add separately cooked whole grains such as buckwheat, rice, wheat or barley to any pan of vegetables that you plan to simmer or *sauté*.

Steaming Vegetables

The simplest steamer consists of a saucepan with a rack inside it so that the food does not touch the water. The further the food is from the water the better. Put about an inch of water in the saucepan and position the rack, ensuring that it stands above the water level. Add the vegetables, cover and bring to the boil.

It is most economical to steam vegetables together. Use a compartmentalized steamer if you have one. Otherwise, arrange the vegetables in groups or layers, make a well for small things like peas, or find a container with holes in it to suit.

Add cauliflower, mushrooms and peas five minutes after other vegetables. Cover again and leave to simmer. Do not let the water boil rapidly as the pot may be boiled dry and the food's nutrients damaged. Most vegetables will be cooked sufficiently in ten minutes. Remove the steamer from the heat. Gently remove the vegetables and save the water for soup or sauce stock. Put it in a covered container in a cold place if you cannot use it at the same meal.

Sautéeing Vegetables

This means cooking gently in a little butter or vegetable oil in an open pan, stirring occasionally. This method seals the surface of the vegetables and so stops vital juices draining away. Any vegetable may be *sautéed* in small pieces. Many more complicated recipes begin by *sautéeing*, especially onions and garlic.

Prepare the vegetables by washing, scrubbing or peeling. Then dice them. Mushrooms, though, are generally *sautéed* whole or sliced, while peppers are cut into sticks or rings and tomatoes into wedges or slices.

Place a little vegetable oil such as sunflower, safflower, olive, corn or soya oil in the pan. One tablespoonful is enough for three large vegetables. Heat the pan slowly and when you see a little blue (not black) smoke rising, add the vegetables. Stir them gently to coat their surfaces with oil, then leave them to cook, stirring to turn them over occasionally. Reduce the heat if necessary. Do not let the cooking be too quick—a gentle bubbling sound only.

Some recipes require that the vegetables be browned, most that the edges turn light gold. Onions are best when they are turning transparent. Experience is very important with *sautéeing* and as you practise you will develop an instinct that tells you when to stir and when to remove food from the heat. Always add vegetables that need least heat last, e.g. mushrooms.

Sautéeing and Steaming (my favourite method)

Use a pan with a well-fitting lid. *Sauté* the vegetables as above and when they are just golden add any herbs and seasoning, then cover them and turn the heat down very low. Even carrots will be cooked in fifteen minutes by this method. I use it mainly with a mixture of vegetables, adding those that need least cooking last. Cauliflower and cabbage, peas and beans are best added just before the lid is put on because they do not *sauté* very well.

Cooking Beans

Choose any combination of beans: haricot, navy beans, soya, black-eyed, aduki, red kidney beans or chick peas, but check that they are not chemically treated. All these are delicious if well soaked (about 6-12 hours) in cold water and then gently boiled in fresh water. Do take care, though, to boil the beans rapidly for at least ten minutes of their cooking time.

Watch the cooking carefully, testing frequently, as they taste best when crisp, rather than soggy and soft. I prefer to cook the beans alone then add them to the other ingredients as the amount of cooking they require tends to kill the flavour of other ingredients if they are cooked together.

Mong dhall, separately soaked for twenty minutes and cooked for ten minutes, will go well with many bean dishes, but, again, do not allow the dhall to go mushy, unless serving as a sambal with curry.

Add beans to risottos, Paprika 'Beef' (tvp) and chilli, Savoury Curry Sauce, or any vegetable dish with only a few ingredients. Avoid mixing beans with starchy foods or sulphurous vegetables (e.g. cabbage, onion, cauliflower).

Cooking Lentils

Wash the lentils well and remove any small stones. Drain, and simmer in fresh water, starting from cold, for about 15-20 minutes. There are red and green types and they may be added to most tvp and vegetable stews.

Salads

The enemy of salads is the loss of nutrients through oxidation. A dressing, though, helps prevent the loss of vitamin value and also enhances flavours. I always toss salad gently in a dressing as soon as it is made.

Always prepare your salad as close as possible to eating time; even at the table if the meal is to be long, leisurely and the conversation flowing. Remember that the smaller the area of cut, peeled or scraped surface of the food the better. Ideally, serve whole fruit or vegetables. As a second best, cut them into wedges or strips; and third on the list of preference, grate or shred them.

Don't forget to consider the appearance of salads. Experiment with graduations of one colour and harmonies of complementary colours. Combine pale and delicate shades with exciting, vibrantly coloured fruit and vegetables.

Shape is important. When there are good colour contrasts, cut everything the same way, but with a limited number of ingredients, cut everything differently. Experiment with the same types of vegetable, using root, leaf and stalk, and cut similarly or differently into wedges, rings, circles, sticks, cubes, oblongs and triangles. Always cut to highlight the particular beauty of the food.

A variety of texture is essential to the good appearance and taste. Try smooth, rough and crisp-textured foods in salads. If you make a habit of considering the beauty of each food you use, you will find salad preparation and eating simply a joy.

For cutting, use a knife that is easy to sharpen, and experiment with chopping boards. You really need a big board and one that will not retain smells. I use an old marble slab.

Salad bowls should be big to make it easy to toss the salad thoroughly. Old-fashioned simple china mixing bowls are ideal, and wooden bowls are very pleasing to the eye as they harmonize in colour and texture with any food, and tossing spoons do not make scraping noises. Remember, though, never to immerse wood in hot soapy water; and seal new bowls with vegetable oil. Clean them with a damp cloth, and be meticulous. Some people like to rub a new wooden bowl with a cut clove of garlic to season it.

Add the unexpected to your salads. For instance: dried fruit (plump it out first by soaking in water); seeds (sesame and sunflower-seeds may be added to any salad except a very rich fatty one with lots of avocado); caraway and fennel (a very light sprinkling just before serving); flowers and weeds (nasturtium flowers or dandelion leaves). Freshly shelled raw nuts also combine very well with most salads, but not with rich oily types. Brazils are surprisingly good. Use peanuts sparingly, though, because they are so acid; and cashews, although delicious raw, are better for you lightly roasted.

Most fresh young vegetables are even better raw than cooked. Never cook cauliflower or cabbage for salads. I hate to say it, but peas and beans are more healthful if gently cooked, and cooked carrot gives a little more carotene than raw, but only a little. Potatoes may also be grated raw into salads occasionally. This way they preserve their considerable vitamin C content.

Sprouting Seeds

Learning to sprout seeds is a satisfying experience combining the gardener's pleasure in watching things grow with that of producing fine, fresh greens all year round. I approached the task of sprouting with trepidation, considering it an expert's job, but I have found that simply does it. Try for yourself. You will find that each type of seed has its own peculiarity, but all will flourish.

First, soak the seeds for 12-24 hours in warm water. Then drain well, spread the seeds over a dish, cover with a cloth and leave in a warm, dark place. Rinse and drain once or twice every 24 hours whilst they are growing. After about a day the sprouts will begin to shoot, so gradually move them into the light so that after three or four days they are growing rapidly and greening. Eat them at any stage after they sprout. Some people like large, green crops at seven days, others prefer small, pale and crunchy sprouts at three to four days.

I use them mostly in salads, but occasionally I lightly steam the more robust kinds, like lentil and aduki, or add them to a curry, casserole or omelette for just a minute or so. Sprouting seeds enhances their nutritional value so that they provide all the essential amino acid constituents, and fruitarians are very keen on them as a source of chlorophyll.

SPRING

Menu Suggestions

1.

Breakfast
Fresh tomatoes on wholemeal toast with butter and freshly ground black pepper

Lunch
Beetroot Soup (p. 22)
Salad of fennel, celery, carrots and watercress
Brie or any other soft cheese

Dinner
Eggs Florentine (p. 40)
New potatoes
Banana and Apple Zesty Salad (p. 55)

2.

Breakfast
Grapefruit and a boiled egg or fresh raspberries and strawberries

Lunch
Rice salad with Edam cheese, carrot, celery, Chinese leaves, served with wedges of tomato and onions

Dinner
Seasonal Vegetables in Savoury Sauce (p. 49)
Cottage Cheese and Apple (p. 56)

3.
Breakfast
Grapes, apple and banana with sunflower seeds and yogurt (p. 112)

Lunch
Cream of Cauliflower Soup (p. 22)
Lettuce, tomato and cucumber salad with a cheese board

Dinner
Baked Eggs (p. 21)
Peanut Bake (p. 45) and steamed fresh vegetables

4.
Breakfast
Dried fruit (soaked overnight) with fresh apple slices and a little cream or yogurt

Lunch
Egg Mayonnaise Roll (p. 24)
Celery and carrot sticks, cucumber slices, tomato wedges and watercress
Wholemeal bread and butter with *Barmene* or *Tastex*

Dinner
Baked Omelette (of leeks and tomatoes) (p. 36)
New potatoes and French beans
Fruit Shortcake (p. 58)

5.
Breakfast
Orange juice, wholemeal toast with tahini and honey

Lunch
Creamed Celery Soup (p. 23)
Tomato, watercress or cabbage and grated Swiss cheese
Fresh fruit with a few almonds and sultanas

Dinner
Lentil Pancakes with Parsley Sauce (p. 44)
Green and Gold Fruit Salad (p. 58)

6.

Breakfast
Grapes, apple and banana

Lunch
Sprouting broccoli, steamed and sprinkled with cheese or butter
Wholemeal bread

Dinner
Spring Minestrone (p. 25)
Savoury Haricot Pie (p. 48)
Fresh cherries or raspberries

7.

Breakfast
Yogurt (p. 112), wheatgerm and honey

Lunch
Watercress Soup (p. 28)
Wholemeal bread and cheese with radishes, cucumber and tomatoes, celery and new
carrots on a platter

Dinner
Slow Omelette (p. 50) using fresh peas or beans and onion
New potatoes
Honeydew Spicy Salad (p. 59)

8.

Breakfast
Peanut butter on wholemeal toast and apple

Lunch
Tomato Soup (p. 26)
Cucumber and apple with mint and yogurt (p. 112)
Toasted almonds and cashews with dried fruit

Dinner
Lentil and Cheese Roast (p. 43)
Carrots and greens
Fresh fruit

9.
Breakfast
Citrus *compote*

Lunch
Celery with lactic or cottage cheese and brown rice or new potatoes

Dinner
Topped Tomatoes (p. 26)
Spinach Pancakes in Cheese Sauce (p. 51)
Grapes or soft fruit

10.
Breakfast
Half grapefruit and/or apple
Wholemeal bread and peanut butter

Lunch
Avocado with tomato, mint and garlic served with French dressing (p. 171)
or
Cabbage and Cashew Salad (p. 29)

Dinner
Steamed broccoli tossed in butter
Leeks and Pasta in Tomato Sauce (p. 42)
Apple and Mint Salad (p. 53)

11.
Breakfast
Poached egg on wholemeal toast
Orange

Lunch
Spinach Cream Soup (p. 24)
Carrot and apple with cheese and walnuts

Dinner
Asparagus Pancakes (p. 21)
Green Risotto (p. 41)
Orange and Date Salad (p. 59)

12.
Breakfast
Banana, pineapple and raisins or sultanas
Wholewheat crispbread and *Tartex pâté*

Lunch
Spring Bean Salad (p. 31) with wholemeal bread and butter
Cottage Cheese Tortoni (p. 57)

Dinner
Watercress Soup (p. 28)
Bean, Tomato and Vegetable Casserole (p. 37)

13.
Breakfast
Grapefruit and poached or scrambled egg on wholemeal toast

Lunch
Tomato and Onion Pancakes (p. 25)
Pineapple, mint and yogurt (p. 112)

Dinner
Potato Salad (p. 31)
Pepper Platter (p. 30) with a cheese board
Rhubarb Fool (p. 61)

14.
Breakfast
Nut and Seed Muesli (p. 59)
Fresh fruit

Lunch
Carrot and celery with cheese
or
Cucumber, cabbage, beetroot and apple in yogurt (p. 112)

Dinner
Chick Pea Roast (p. 38) with green peas and carrots
Topped Tomatoes (p. 26)
Grape Fruit Salad (p. 58)

Starters

ASPARAGUS PANCAKES

Roll up hot asparagus tips in hot pancakes (basic recipe, page 141) and brush the tops with butter. Sprinkle with sea salt, freshly ground black pepper and lemon juice.

BAKED EGGS

1. Butter a few individual ovenproof dishes and make a nest of one of the following mixtures in each dish:

    Soft breadcrumbs mixed with fried onion, peppers or grated cheese;
    Cauliflower or another vegetable in a thick sauce;
    Beans in tomato sauce (see recipe, page 175);
    Mashed potato, cottage cheese and *fines herbes*;
    Sautéed onions, tomatoes and mushrooms.

2. Into each nest, gently break one egg. Season and cover the egg with one of the following:

    Soured cream;
    Breadcrumbs dotted with butter;
    Grated cheese;
    Cheese or white sauce;
    Sautéed mushrooms.

3. Bake the eggs at 400°F/200°C (Gas Mark 6) for 10 minutes. Serve hot with a green salad.

BEETROOT SOUP

Imperial (Metric)	American
1 lb (½ kilo) potatoes, diced	1 lb potatoes diced
1 lb (½ kilo) onions, diced	1 lb onions, diced
1 lb (½ kilo) beetroot, freshly cooked and diced	1 lb beetroot, freshly cooked and diced
2 oz (50g) butter	¼ cupful butter
2-3 pints (1-1½ litres) vegetable stock	5-7½ cupsful vegetable stock
¼ pint (150ml) double or soured cream	¾ cupful double or soured cream
1 wineglassful dry red wine	1 wineglassful dry red wine

1. Melt the butter in the saucepan and *sauté* the potatoes and onions for 10 minutes.

2. Add the beetroot and cook gently for a further 5 minutes without browning the vegetables.

3. Add the stock, bring to the boil, then simmer the soup for half an hour.

4. Sieve or liquidize the mixture to a *purée*, then reheat and add the wine and cream just before serving, either hot or cold. (Alternatively, omit the cream and wine and use ½ pint / ¼ litre of milk.)

CREAM OF CAULIFLOWER SOUP

Imperial (Metric)	American
1 medium-sized cauliflower, firm and white	1 medium-sized cauliflower, firm and white
½ oz (15g) butter	1 tablespoonful butter
½ pint (¼ litre) vegetable stock	1¼ cupsful vegetable stock
1 large onion, diced	1 large onion, diced
1 dessertspoonful fresh rosemary, chopped	1 tablespoonful fresh rosemary, chopped

1. Break the cauliflower into florets and steam it in a little water until well cooked but still crisp.

2. Meanwhile, melt the butter in a heavy saucepan and *sauté* the onion.

3. Add the stock, then the rosemary and simmer gently. When the cauliflower is ready, add the cooking water to the stock.

4. Rub the cauliflower through a sieve and combine the *purée* with the stock. Alternatively, blend all the ingredients.

5. Return the soup to the saucepan and simmer gently for 5-10 minutes, adjusting the seasoning as necessary.

CREAMED CELERY SOUP

Imperial (Metric)
1 large head celery
1 large onion, diced or
1 small onion and 1 leek, diced
2 pints (1 litre) vegetable stock
1 oz (25g) butter
1 oz (25g) wholemeal flour
¼ pint (150ml) milk
¼ pint (150ml) cream
1 tablespoonful parsley, freshly chopped
Freshly ground black pepper and bouquet garni

American
1 large head celery
1 large onion, diced or
1 small onion and 1 leek, diced
5 cupsful vegetable stock
2½ tablespoonsful butter
¼ cupful wholemeal flour
¾ cupful milk
¾ cupful cream
1 tablespoonful parsley, freshly chopped
Freshly ground black pepper and bouquet garni

1. Prepare the celery in half inch slices, reserving the heart for a salad and a few of the best slices for a garnish.

2. Melt the butter in a saucepan, add the celery and onions and *sauté* them for a few minutes until tender.

3. Add the stock and bouquet garni and simmer for half an hour. Allow to cool slightly and then *purée* the mixture in a liquidizer or pass through a sieve or plastic sieve. (If using a liquidizer, pass the mixture through a sieve as well to ensure that all the stringy bits are discarded.)

4. Return the mixture to the saucepan and heat slowly.

5. Mix a little of the milk with the flour to make a paste and gradually add the remaining milk.

6. Pour the milk onto the *purée* and heat slowly to boiling point.

7. Boil the soup for two minutes, remove from the heat, then add the cream.

8. Adjust the seasoning, garnish with diced or finely sliced celery and sprinkle with the parsley.

EGG MAYONNAISE ROLL

Imperial (Metric)
4 hard-boiled eggs, chopped
½ lb (¼ kilo) Cheddar cheese, grated
6 gherkins or to taste
6 olives or to taste
2 tablespoonful chopped chives, spring
  onions or onion
1 teaspoonful mustard
2 tablespoonful mayonnaise (page 172)
2 tablespoonful cream
Sea salt and freshly ground black pepper

American
4 hard-boiled eggs, chopped
2⅔ cupful Cheddar cheese, grated
6 gherkins or to taste
6 olives or to taste
2½ tablespoonful chopped chives, spring
  onions or onion
1 teaspoonful mustard
2½ tablespoonful mayonnaise (page 172)
2½ tablespoonful cream
Sea salt and freshly ground black pepper

1. Combine all the ingredients, dampen the hands and form the mixture into a roll. Wrap the roll in clingfilm and chill for at least one hour.

2. Cut the roll into slices and serve in crackers or with a salad platter.

SPINACH CREAM SOUP

Imperial (Metric)
1 lb (½ kilo) spinach
3 oz (75g) butter
1-2 oz (25-50g) wholemeal flour
¼ pint (150ml) double or single cream
  (optional)
Pinch of nutmeg, freshly grated
2 oz (50g) Cheddar, Gouda or Swiss cheese,
  grated
Sea salt and freshly ground black pepper

American
1 lb spinach
½ cupful butter
¼-½ cupful wholemeal flour
¾ cupful double or single cream
  (optional)
Pinch of nutmeg, freshly grated
½ cupful Cheddar, Gouda or Swiss cheese,
  grated
Sea salt and freshly ground black pepper

1. Trim, wash and drain the spinach and cook it very gently in a covered pan with 1 oz (25g) of the butter.

2. Pass the spinach through a sieve or liquidizer, reserving any liquid.

3. Meanwhile, melt the butter, add the flour and cook the mixture over a low heat for 1-2 minutes.

4. Gradually add the spinach and its juice. (If the soup is too thick, add a little milk.)

5. Season well and stir in the cream. Pour the soup into warm bowls and sprinkle cheese over the top.

SPRING MINESTRONE

Imperial (Metric)
½ lb (¼ kilo) broad beans
½ lb (¼ kilo) peas
3 sticks celery, chopped
1 onion, sliced
1 clove garlic, crushed (optional)
½ lb (¼ kilo) tomatoes, peeled and quartered
½ lb (¼ kilo) spinach, roughly chopped
2 carrots, diced
4 oz (100g) brown rice (raw)
Pinch each of basil and marjoram
2 tablespoonsful parsley, freshly chopped
3 pints (1½ litres) water or vegetable stock
4 oz (100g) Parmesan cheese, grated
Vecon or yeast extract to taste
Sea salt and freshly ground black pepper

American
1½ cupsful broad beans
1½ cupsful peas
3 sticks celery, chopped
1 onion, sliced
1 clove garlic, crushed (optional)
2 cupsful tomatoes, peeled and quartered
½ lb spinach, roughly chopped
2 carrots, diced
1 cupful brown rice (raw)
Pinch each of basil and marjoram
2½ tablespoonsful parsley, freshly chopped
7½ cupsful water or vegetable stock
1 cupful Parmesan cheese, grated
Vecon or yeast extract to taste
Sea salt and freshly ground black pepper

1. Add all the vegetables, rice and herbs to the stock.

2. Simmer the soup gently for 1 hour, stirring occasionally.

3. Stir in the cheese before serving, and season to taste.

TOMATO AND ONION PANCAKES

Imperial (Metric)
1 lb (½ kilo) tomatoes, peeled and sliced
2 large onions, diced
1 oz (25g) butter
1 tablespoonful cider vinegar
Pinch of sweet basil and dry mustard
Freshly ground black pepper

American
1 lb tomatoes, peeled and sliced
2 large onions, diced
2½ tablespoonsful butter
1 tablespoonful cider vinegar
Pinch of sweet basil and dry mustard
Freshly ground black pepper

8 pancakes (page 141).

1. *Sauté* the onions and add the tomatoes to the pan. Season and cook gently.

2. Fill the pancakes with the tomatoes and onions and, if liked, top with mushrooms *sautéed* in butter or with cheese sauce; grill to brown the top.

TOMATO SOUP

Imperial (Metric)	American
1 onion, diced	1 onion, diced
1 clove garlic, crushed	1 clove garlic, crushed
2 tablespoonful butter	2½ tablespoonful butter
1 lb (½ kilo) tomatoes, skinned and roughly chopped	1 lb tomatoes, skinned and roughly chopped
1½ pints (¾ litre) water	3¾ cupsful water
Bouquet garni	Bouquet garni
Sea salt and freshly ground black pepper	Sea salt and freshly ground black pepper

1. *Sauté* the onion and garlic in the butter. Add the tomatoes, seasoning and bouquet garni and cook for a minute or two, stirring gently.

2. Add the water, cover the saucepan and simmer the soup for 20-30 minutes.

3. Remove the bouquet garni, allow the soup to cool and then liquidize or sieve it.

4. Add a little tomato paste if liked, but if so, omit the salt. Serve this soup sprinkled with fresh parsley or with a dash of cream or dry sherry. Alternatively, serve chilled, garnished with slices of cucumber or lemon.

TOPPED TOMATOES

Imperial (Metric)	American
4 firm red tomatoes	4 firm red tomatoes
3 tablespoonful fresh wholemeal breadcrumbs	4 tablespoonful fresh wholemeal breadcrumbs
1 clove garlic, crushed	1 clove garlic, crushed
2-3 spring onions, chopped	2-3 spring onions, chopped
A large pinch of mixed herbs	A large pinch of mixed herbs
Fresh parsley, chopped (turns the mixture green)	Fresh parsley, chopped (turns the mixture green)
Nut of butter, melted	Nut of butter, melted
Sea salt and freshly ground black pepper	Sea salt and freshly ground black pepper

1. Halve the tomatoes and arrange them in an ovenproof dish.

2. Combine the remaining ingredients and top each tomato with some of the mixture.

3. Bake for 20 minutes at 350°F/180°C (Gas Mark 4).

VEGETABLE SOUP

Basic Stock:

Imperial (Metric)
1½ pints (¾ litre) water
1 onion, chopped
1 carrot, chopped
1 turnip, chopped
1 bay leaf
Tender leaves of cabbage or cauliflower,
   chopped
Sea salt and freshly ground black pepper

American
3¾ cupsful water
1 onion, chopped
1 carrot, chopped
1 turnip, chopped
1 bay leaf
Tender leaves of cabbage or cauliflower,
   chopped
Sea salt and freshly ground black pepper

1. Simmer the ingredients in a covered pan for ½-¾ hour. Cool and strain to use as stock.

Optional Ingredients:

   1 onion, diced;
   Tomatoes, skinned and cut into wedges;
   Celery, sliced;
   Carrots, cut into sticks or rings;
   Potatoes, diced;
   Mushrooms, whole or halved;
   Barley and lentils.

1. *Sauté* the onion in a little butter. Add any combination of the ingredients listed above and cook for a few minutes, stirring gently.

2. Cover the vegetables with the strained stock and simmer for 25 minutes. (At this point, bean sprouts or shredded cabbage may be added to the soup and cooked for another 5 minutes.)

3. Check the seasoning, *purée* the soup if desired or leave the vegetables whole. Garnish with chopped parsley or serve with a dish of grated cheese, preferably Parmesan.

WATERCRESS SOUP

Imperial (Metric)
1-2 bunches watercress, washed thoroughly
1 large onion, diced
1 clove garlic, crushed (optional)
2 large potatoes, diced
2 oz (50g) butter
1 pint (½ litre) vegetable stock
¾ pint (400ml) milk
¼ pint (150ml) single cream

American
1-2 bunches watercress, washed thoroughly
1 large onion, diced
1 clove garlic, crushed (optional)
2 large potatoes, diced
¼ cupful butter
2½ cupsful vegetable stock
1¾ cupsful milk
¾ cupful single cream

1. *Sauté* the onion, garlic and potato until golden, then add half of the stock. Cover the pan and simmer the stock for 30 minutes.

2. Meanwhile, finely chop the stems and about half the leaves of the watercress. Add them to the stock. Simmer for a further 15 minutes, then sieve or liquidize the soup.

3. Season to taste, add the milk and remaining stock and reheat the soup.

4. Add the cream just before serving or pour it into the bowls over the soup.

Salads and Salad Dressings

CABBAGE AND CASHEW SALAD

Imperial (Metric)
1 small cabbage, sliced
1 onion, diced (optional)
2 peppers—1 green, 1 red, sliced
2 small apples—1 green, 1 red, sliced
3 oz (75g) sultanas or currants
3 oz (75g) whole cashew nuts, unsalted
5 oz (150g) cooked brown rice (optional)

American
1 small cabbage, sliced
1 onion, diced (optional)
2 peppers—1 green, 1 red, sliced
2 small apples—1 green, 1 red, sliced
⅔ cupful sultanas or currants
¾ cupful whole cashew nuts, unsalted
2 cupsful cooked brown rice (optional)

1. Combine all the ingredients using an oil and vinegar, yogurt or tomato dressing, (pages 30, 32 and 86). (The nuts taste particularly good if gently roasted in a moderate oven until golden. Hazelnuts may be used instead of cashews.)

HARICOT SALAD

Imperial (Metric)
1 lb (½ kilo) well cooked haricot beans
½-¾ lb (225-350g) tomatoes, sliced
1 large clove garlic, crushed
1 large green pepper, sliced
2-3 tablespoonsful fresh parsley, chopped

American
2½ cupsful navy beans, well cooked
1½ cupsful tomatoes, sliced
1 large clove garlic, crushed
1 large green pepper, sliced
3 tablespoonsful fresh parsley, chopped

1. Combine all the ingredients and toss the salad in French dressing (page 171).

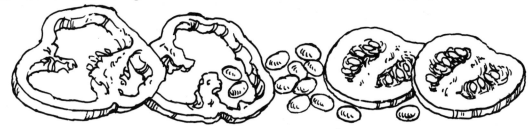

OIL AND VINEGAR DRESSING

Imperial (Metric)
4 tablespoonsful vegetable oil
1-2 tablespoonsful cider vinegar
Pinch each of dry mustard and *fines herbes*
Dash of *Tabasco* sauce
Raw cane sugar to taste
Sea salt and freshly ground black pepper

American
5 tablespoonsful vegetable oil
1-2 tablespoonsful cider vinegar
Pinch each of dry mustard and *fines herbes*
Dash of *Tabasco* sauce
Raw cane sugar to taste
Sea salt and freshly ground black pepper

1. Blend the ingredients thoroughly.

PEPPER AND TOMATO SALAD

Imperial (Metric)
1 lb (½ kilo) red and green peppers,
  sliced thickly
¾ lb (350g) tomatoes, cut into wedges
1 medium-sized onion, sliced finely (optional)

American
1 lb red and green peppers, sliced
  thickly
¾ lb tomatoes, cut into wedges
1 medium-sized onion, sliced finely (optional)

1. Combine the ingredients with oil and vinegar dressing (page 30), adding a pinch of rosemary and marjoram. Celery may be used to replace the onion as a variation.

PEPPER PLATTER

Imperial (Metric)
1 lb (½ kilo) green and red peppers, cut into
  broad slices
3 medium-sized carrots, cut into long sticks
3 sticks celery, sliced into 3 in. pieces
1 small onion, diced very finely
2 tablespoonsful parsley, chopped

American
1 lb green and red peppers, cut into broad
  slices
3 medium-sized carrots, cut into long sticks
3 sticks celery, sliced into 3 in. pieces
1 small onion, diced very finely
2½ tablespoonsful parsley, chopped

1. Arrange the vegetables on a flat dish and sprinkle the onion and parsley over them. Serve instead of crackers with cheese dips.

POTATO SALAD

Imperial (Metric)
1 lb (½ kilo) new potatoes, scrubbed, cooked
  whole and diced
1-2 onions, diced or sliced into rings
½ medium-sized cauliflower, cut into florets
1 tablespoonful fresh mint, chopped
Large pinch of dried rosemary or
1 teaspoonful fresh rosemary, chopped
Freshly grated nutmeg

American
1 lb new potatoes, scrubbed, cooked whole and
  diced
1-2 onions, diced or sliced into rings
½ medium-sized cauliflower, cut into florets
1 tablespoonful fresh mint, chopped
Large pinch of dried rosemary or
1 teaspoonful fresh rosemary, chopped
Freshly grated nutmeg

1. Combine the ingredients with a generous helping of soured cream, French dressing (page 171) or mayonnaise (page 172).

PULSE SALAD

Imperial (Metric)
¾ lb (350g) pulses, well cooked but still crisp
3-4 spring onions, sliced into rings
4 oz (100g) mushrooms, sliced
1 green apple, diced
1 red or green pepper, sliced
6 oz (200g) sunflower or sesame seeds

American
1¾ cupful pulses, well cooked but still crisp
3-4 spring onions, sliced into rings
2 cupful mushrooms, sliced
1 green apple, diced
1 red or green pepper, sliced
1 cupful sunflower or sesame seeds

1. Any combination of pulses may be used in this salad, for example:

   Soya beans with Continental lentils;
   Haricot beans with soya, aduki or red kidney beans;
   Black-eyed beans with lentils.

2. Combine the ingredients with a French or tomato dressing, (pages 171 and 86).

SPRING BEAN SALAD

Combine 1 lb (½ kilo) of green beans, sliced and steamed, with one bunch of spring onions, sliced into rings. Toss the salad in an oil and vinegar dressing (page 30), mixed with one teaspoonful of paprika.

YOGURT DRESSING

1. Yogurt, tomato paste, lemon juice, raw cane sugar, sea salt and freshly ground black pepper.

2. Yogurt, a little honey, cider vinegar, sea salt, freshly ground black pepper and a strong herb, e.g. basil.

3. Yogurt may also be served on its own as a salad dressing.

Savoury Dishes

ALMOND AND ONION LOAF

Imperial (Metric)
4 oz (100g) ground almonds
4 oz (100g) wholemeal breadcrumbs
2 onions, diced
1 tablespoonful vegetable oil
1 egg, beaten
Nutmeg and marjoram to taste
Sea salt and freshly ground black pepper

American
1 cupful ground almonds
2½ cupsful wholemeal breadcrumbs
2 onions, diced
1 tablespoonful vegetable oil
1 egg, beaten
Nutmeg and marjoram to taste
Sea salt and freshly ground black pepper

1. *Sauté* the onions in the oil, allow them to cool slightly and then add them to the remaining ingredients.

2. Place the mixture in a shallow greased dish, top with slices of tomato and an almond on each slice.

3. Bake for 30 minutes at 350°F/180°C (Gas Mark 4).

BAKED BUTTER BEANS AND CHEESE

Imperial (Metric)
¾ lb (350g) butter beans, soaked and drained
1 onion, sliced
1 clove garlic, crushed
2 carrots, sliced
2 sticks celery, sliced
2 oz (50g) butter
½ medium-sized tin tomatoes
2 tablespoonsful fresh parsley, chopped
1 teaspoonful each tomato *purée* and yeast
  extract
1 vegetable stock cube
Dash of soy sauce
Freshly ground black pepper and chilli powder
Bouquet garni

American
1½ cupsful navy beans, soaked and drained
1 onion, sliced
1 clove garlic, crushed
2 carrots, sliced
2 sticks celery, sliced
¼ cupful butter
½ medium-sized tin tomatoes
2½ tablespoonsful fresh parsley, chopped
1 teaspoonful each tomato *purée* and yeast
  extract
1 vegetable stock cube
Dash of soy sauce
Freshly ground black pepper and chilli powder
Bouquet garni

Topping:

4 oz (100g) grated cheese
2 tablespoonsful sesame seeds
2-3 tablespoonsful wheat germ or breadcrumbs

1½ cupsful grated cheese
2½ tablespoonsful sesame seeds
3 tablespoonsful wheat germ or breadcrumbs

1. Fry the onion, garlic, carrot and celery in the butter for 10 minutes.

2. Stir in the beans, add the bouquet garni and the stock cube.

3. Cover with water to half an inch above the ingredients, bring to the boil for 10 minutes, adding a little more water if necessary, and then simmer, covered, for 1¼ hours until the beans are tender.

4. Remove the bouquet garni, add the remaining ingredients and mix well.

5. Turn the mixture into a greased ovenproof dish and top with the cheese, seeds and breadcrumbs or wheat germ. Bake for 30 minutes at 350°F/180°C (Gas Mark 4).

SPRING

Spring Minestrone (page 25)
Avocado and Lime Delight (page 55)
Savoury Crumble (page 46)
Pepper Platter (page 30)

BAKED OMELETTE

Imperial (Metric)

American

For each person use:

1 egg
1 tablespoonful yogurt or milk
2 tablespoonsful grated cheese (optional)
Herbs to complement the type of omelette
Sea salt and freshly ground black pepper

1 egg
1 tablespoonful yogurt or milk
2½ tablespoonsful grated cheese (optional)
Herbs to complement the type of omelette
Sea salt and freshly ground black pepper

1. Blend the ingredients together, adding the cheese last.

2. Pour the mixture into a buttered stoneware or pottery ovenproof dish, covering one of the following:

    Cooked asparagus;
    Sautéed onions and mushrooms;
    Sautéed onions, carrots, potato and mushrooms with green beans and peppers;
    Lightly steamed seasonal vegetables;
    Sweet corn and peppers;
    Sautéed courgettes, mushrooms, onions and tomatoes.

3. Garnish the omelette with one of the following:

    Grated cheese, sunflower or sesame seeds;
    Soft wholemeal breadcrumbs dotted with butter;
    Large mushrooms;
    Tomato slices.

4. Bake in a moderate oven at 350°F/180°C (Gas Mark 4) for about 40 minutes, increasing the heat a little towards the end to brown the top.

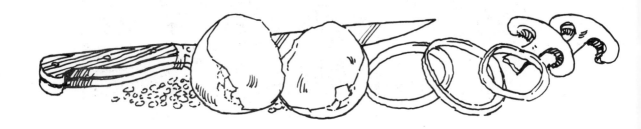

BEAN, TOMATO AND VEGETABLE CASSEROLE

Imperial (Metric)
1½ lb (¾ kilo) beans, well cooked
1 large onion, diced
2-3 carrots, cut into rings or sticks
2 sticks celery, chopped
4 oz (100g) mushrooms
4 oz (100g) bean sprouts
6 small cauliflower florets or
4 oz (100g) fresh green peas
2-3 tablespoonful tomato paste
1 teaspoonful *Marmite* or *Vecon* (optional)
¼ pint (150ml) vegetable stock (or water reserved from cooking beans)
1 bay leaf
Pinch of oregano and paprika
Sea salt and freshly ground black pepper

American
3 cupful beans, well cooked
1 large onion, diced
2-3 carrots, cut into rings or sticks
2 sticks celery, chopped
2 cupful mushrooms
2 cupful bean sprouts
6 small cauliflower florets or
1½ cupful fresh green peas
3 tablespoonful tomato paste
1 teaspoonful *Marmite* or *Vecon* (optional)
¾ cupful vegetable stock (or water reserved from cooking beans)
1 bay leaf
Pinch of oregano and paprika
Sea salt and freshly ground black pepper

1. *Sauté* the onion and carrots, add the celery, tomatoes, tomato paste and seasonings, and mix well.

2. Cook for about 5 minutes then pour on the stock or water. Add the beans, cover the pan and cook very slowly for 20 minutes.

3. Add the mushrooms and cauliflower or green peas, cover the pan and simmer until almost cooked.

4. Add the bean sprouts, check the seasoning and cook for 2 more minutes. Serve with grated cheese.

BEANS IN CHEESE AND ONION SAUCE

Take any combination of beans, cooked until soft but still crisp. Arrange them in a buttered dish and cover with cheese sauce (page 136) to which has been added 1 large onion, grated. Top with mixed grated cheese and breadcrumbs and brown well in a moderate oven at 350°F/180°C (Gas Mark 4) for about 30 minutes.

CAULIFLOWER AND POTATO CURRY

Imperial (Metric)
2 potatoes, peeled and cut into 1 in. cubes
1 small cauliflower, cut into florets
4 oz (100g) butter
½ teaspoonful cumin
1 teaspoonful turmeric
Pinch of chilli powder
Freshly grated root ginger
Sea salt and freshly ground black pepper

American
2 potatoes, peeled and cut into 1 in. cubes
1 small cauliflower, cut into florets
½ cupful butter
½ teaspoonful cumin
1 teaspoonful turmeric
Pinch of chilli powder
Freshly grated root ginger
Sea salt and freshly ground black pepper

1. Heat the butter and add all the ingredients except the cauliflower. Fry the vegetables for 2 minutes, then add the florets and cook for 5 minutes more.

2. Reduce the heat, cover the pan and simmer for 5 minutes. Sprinkle the curry with pepper before serving, accompanied by sambals (page 142).

CHICK PEA ROAST

Imperial (Metric)
½ lb (¼ kilo) chick peas, soaked overnight
2 tablespoonsful tomato paste or *Tastex*
1 egg to bind
1 oz (25g) butter or vegetable oil

American
1 cupful garbanzo beans, soaked overnight
2½ tablespoonsful tomato paste or *Tastex*
1 egg to bind
2½ tablespoonsful butter or vegetable oil

1. Boil the peas until tender, then drain and grind or mash them until smooth.

2. Add the remaining ingredients to make a tasty paste and place the mixture in an oiled overproof dish. Dot with butter on the top and sprinkle with black pepper.

3. Bake for 40 minutes at 350°F/180°C (Gas Mark 4) and serve with a tomato gravy and vegetables.

SPRING

Green Risotto (page 41)
Asparagus Pancakes (page 21)
Nut and Seed Muesli (page 59)
Cottage Cheese Tortoni (page 57)

EGG AND ONION LOAF

Imperial (Metric)
2 oz (50g) soft wholemeal breadcrumbs
3 oz (75g) cooked brown rice
2 onions, finely diced
3 tablespoonsful vegetable oil
1 egg, lightly beaten
1 teaspoonful soy sauce
3 hard-boiled eggs
2 teaspoonsful herbs (e.g. sage and thyme or
  parsley, sweet basil and marjoram)
Freshly ground black pepper

American
1½ cupsful soft wholemeal breadcrumbs
1 cupful cooked brown rice
2 onions, finely diced
4 tablespoonsful vegetable oil
1 egg, lightly beaten
1 teaspoonful soy sauce
3 hard-boiled eggs
2 teaspoonful herbs (e.g. sage and thyme or
  parsley, sweet basil and marjoram)
Freshly ground black pepper

1. Soften the onions in the oil over a gentle heat. Combine all the ingredients except the eggs.
    (These may be chopped and added, or placed in the middle of the loaf so that they cut into
    rings as you slice the loaf. To do this, place one half of the mixture in an oiled loaf tin,
    arrange the eggs lengthwise along it and cover the eggs with the rest of the mixture.)

2. Garnish the loaf by brushing it with oil and gently pressing dried herbs into the top. Bake
    at 350°F/180°C (Gas Mark 4) for 30 minutes.

EGGS FLORENTINE

Imperial (Metric)
1½ lb (¾ kilo) spinach, well washed and shaken
4 eggs
2 tablespoonsful butter or vegetable oil
A little lemon juice
Sea salt and freshly ground black pepper

American
1½ lb spinach, well washed and shaken
4 eggs
2½ tablespoonsful butter or vegetable oil
A little lemon juice
Sea salt and freshly ground black pepper

1. Cut the spinach and cook it in the butter or oil with the lemon juice and seasoning.

2. In an ovenproof dish, make nests of the spinach and break the eggs into them. Season well
    and cover with cheese or white sauce (page 136).

3. Sprinkle with Parmesan cheese if liked, and bake for 15 minutes at 350°F/180°C (Gas
    Mark 4). (Diced boiled potatoes or cooked brown rice or buckwheat may be added to the
    spinach nests and grated cheese may be used to replace the sauce.)

GREEN RISOTTO

Imperial (Metric)
1½ lb (¾ kilo) spring greens or purple broccoli
  sprouting
1 large onion, diced
1 clove garlic, crushed
2-3 oz (50-75g) cooked brown rice
2 oz (50g) butter
2 oz (50g) whole rice flour
¾ pint (400ml) vegetable water or milk
1-2 tablespoonsful tomato paste
Pinch of basil
Sea salt and freshly ground black pepper

American
1½ lb spring greens or purple broccoli
  sprouting
1 large onion, diced
1 clove garlic, crushed
1¼ cupsful cooked brown rice
¼ cupful butter
½ cupful whole rice flour
1¾ cupsful vegetable water or milk
2 tablespoonsful tomato paste
Pinch of basil
Sea salt and freshly ground black pepper

1. Wash and shred the vegetables, discarding any thick, woody stems.

2. Place the vegetables in a large saucepan with 1 in. of water, the onion and garlic, a large knob of butter and seasoning.

3. Cover the pan and cook the vegetables until tender but still crisp. Place them in a greased ovenproof dish with the rice and mix well.

4. Make the sauce by melting the butter, adding the flour and cooking for 1-2 minutes over a low heat. Add the liquid and seasoning, stirring as the sauce thickens.

5. Pour the sauce over the vegetables and sprinkle sunflower seeds over the top. Bake for 20 minutes in a moderate oven at 350°F/180°C (Gas Mark 4). (The sauce may be enriched with one or two beaten eggs.)

LEEKS AND PASTA IN TOMATO SAUCE

Imperial (Metric)
1½-2 lb (¾-1 kilo) leeks, cut into rings
½ lb (¼ kilo) mushrooms, sliced
6 oz (200g) wholemeal vermicelli
2 oz (50g) wholemeal flour
4 tablespoonsful vegetable oil
1 medium-sized tin tomatoes
½ pint (¼ litre) milk or
¼ pint (150ml) each milk and vegetable stock
  or wine
1 clove garlic, crushed
Pinch of basil, rosemary, nutmeg and oregano
4 oz (100g) Cheddar, Gouda or Gruyère, grated
2 oz (50g) fresh wholemeal breadcrumbs or
  sunflower seeds
Sea salt and freshly ground black pepper

American
1½-2 lb leeks, cut into rings
4 cupsful mushrooms, sliced
6 oz wholemeal vermicelli
½ cupful wholemeal flour
5 tablespoonsful vegetable oil
1 medium-sized tin tomatoes
1¼ cupsful milk or
¾ cupful milk and vegetable stock or
  wine
1 clove garlic, crushed
Pinch of basil, rosemary, nutmeg and oregano
1½ cupsful Cheddar, Gouda or Gruyère, grated
1¼ cupsful or ½ cupful fresh wholemeal
  breadcrumbs or sunflower seeds
Sea salt and freshly ground black pepper

Vegetables:

Vary the vegetable layer according to availability, for example:

1 lb (½ kilo) aubergines, peeled and diced or
1 lb (½ kilo) red and green peppers or
½ lb (¼ kilo) mushrooms

1 lb eggplants or
1 lb red and green peppers or
4 cupsful mushrooms

1. *Sauté* the leeks and mushrooms in half the oil with the nutmeg, pepper and salt. Meanwhile, cook the pasta to the 'chewy' stage.

2. Make a sauce using the rest of the oil, gently heated and mixed with the flour.

3. Remove from the heat and add the leeks, mushrooms and tomatoes. Stir well over a low heat and gradually add the milk, stock or wine.

4. In a deep ovenproof dish, layer the vegetables, half the pasta, half the sauce, the remaining pasta and the remaining sauce. Top with the breadcrumbs or seeds and grated cheese. Bake for 20 minutes at 350°F/180°C (Gas Mark 4) to brown the top.

LENTIL AND CHEESE ROAST

Imperial (Metric)
6 oz (200g) red lentils
1 large onion, diced
1 carrot, grated
2 oz (50g) butter or polyunsaturated
  margarine or
2 tablespoonsful vegetable oil
1½ teaspoonsful yeast extract
1 vegetable stock cube
4 oz (100g) grated cheese
1 egg, beaten
Freshly ground black pepper
Mixed herbs to taste

American
¾ cupful red lentils
1 large onion, diced
1 carrot, grated
¼ cupful butter or polyunsaturated
  margarine or
2½ tablespoonsful vegetable oil
1½ teaspoonsful yeast extract
1 vegetable stock cube
1⅓ cupsful grated cheese
1 egg, beaten
Freshly ground black pepper
Mixed herbs to taste

1. Cook the lentils in water with the stock cube.

2. *Sauté* the onion and carrot in the fat and then combine all the ingredients, adding the egg last.

3. Bake in a well greased ovenproof dish or loaf tin for 30-40 minutes at 375°F/190°C (Gas Mark 5).

LENTIL PANCAKES WITH PARSLEY SAUCE

Prepare the pancakes according to the basic recipe using 4 oz (100g) wholemeal flour.

Filling:

Imperial (Metric)	American
1 onion, diced	1 onion, diced
2 oz (50g) butter	¼ cupful butter
1 teaspoonful vegetable oil	1 teaspoonful vegetable oil
½ lb (¼ kilo) lentils	1 cupful lentils
½ pint (¼ litre) water	1¼ cupsful water
6-8 oz (200g) small mushrooms	3-4 cupsful small mushrooms
1 teaspoonful ground coriander	1 teaspoonful ground coriander
1 vegetable stock cube	1 vegetable stock cube
1 teaspoonful tomato *purée*	1 teaspoonful tomato *purée*
1 small tin tomatoes	1 small tin tomatoes
½ teaspoonful raw cane sugar	½ teaspoonful raw cane sugar
2-3 tablespoonsful red wine	3 tablespoonsful red wine

1. Fry the onion in the butter and vegetable oil for 5 minutes.

2. Add the lentils, stock cube, water, tomatoes, coriander and wine, and simmer gently, uncovered, for 30 minutes until the mixture reduces to a thick pulp.

3. Add the mushrooms and cook for a further 5 minutes.

Sauce:

Imperial (Metric)	American
½ pint (¼ litre) milk	1¼ cupsful milk
¼ pint (150ml) single cream	¾ cupful single cream
1½ oz (40g) butter	3 tablespoonsful butter
1 oz (25g) wholemeal flour	¼ cupful wholemeal flour
3 tablespoonsful fresh parsley, finely chopped	3 tablespoonsful fresh parsley, finely chopped
A little lemon juice	A little lemon juice
¼ vegetable stock cube (optional)	¼ vegetable stock cube (optional)
Freshly ground black pepper	Freshly ground black pepper

1. Make a roux of the flour and butter, cooking for a minute or two over a low heat.

2. Remove from the heat and add the milk, whisking to make a smooth sauce.

3. Add the remaining ingredients and cook very gently for a few minutes.

4. Serve the pancakes in a long dish, covered with the sauce.

PEANUT BAKE

Imperial (Metric)
½ lb (¼ kilo) shelled peanuts, dry roasted in the oven
3 oz (75g) butter or vegetable oil
3 oz (75g) soft wholemeal breadcrumbs
4 tomatoes, skinned and chopped
¼ teaspoonful sage
½ teaspoonful thyme
Dash of cayenne pepper
Sea salt to taste

American
2 cupsful shelled peanuts, dry roasted in the oven
⅓ cupful butter or vegetable oil
2 cupsful soft wholemeal breadcrumbs
4 tomatoes, skinned and chopped
¼ teaspoonful sage
½ teaspoonful thyme
Dash of cayenne pepper
Sea salt to taste

1. Combine the butter or oil with the breadcrumbs and mix the tomatoes and herbs with the peanuts.

2. Sprinkle half of the breadcrumbs onto the base of a greased ovenproof dish, add the peanut mixture and another layer of breadcrumbs.

3. Bake at 350°F/180°C (Gas Mark 4) for 30-40 minutes.

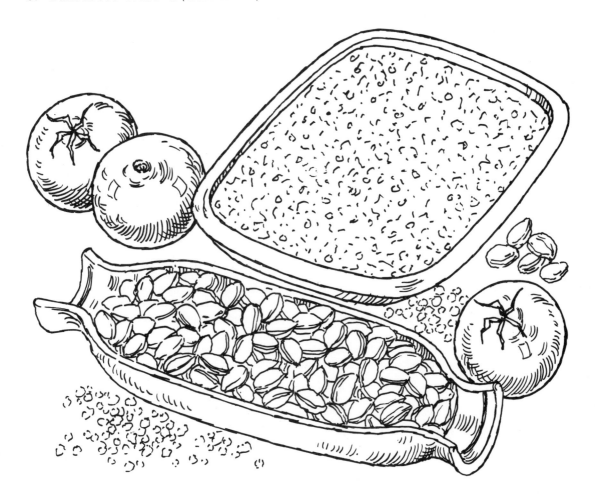

SAVOURY CRUMBLES

Bases:

1.

Imperial (Metric)	American
½ lb (¼ kilo) onions, diced	2 cupsful onions, diced
1 lb (½ kilo) carrots, diced	3 cupsful carrots, diced
1 lb (½ kilo) seasonal vegetables	1 lb seasonal vegetables
½ pint (¼ litre) water	1¼ cupsful water
2 oz (50g) butter	¼ cupful butter
2 oz (50g) wholemeal flour	½ cupful wholemeal flour
1 pint (½ litre) vegetable stock	2½ cupsful vegetable stock
2 tablespoonsful vegetable oil	2½ tablespoonsful vegetable oil
1 tablespoonful tamari sauce or to taste	1 tablespoonful tamari sauce or to taste
Sea salt to taste	Sea salt to taste

1. *Sauté* the vegetables for 5-10 minutes, then add up to ½ pint water and stir until the vegetables are cooked.

2. Melt the butter, add the flour and cook for 1 minute. Gradually add the stock, including the vegetable water. Stir until the mixture thickens.

3. Place the vegetables in an ovenproof baking dish, adjust the seasoning, add the tamari and cover with the sauce. Sprinkle a crumble topping (page 47) liberally over the top.

4. Bake at 350°F/180°C (Gas Mark 4) until the crumble is brown. (I would sometimes add chopped fresh herbs, particularly parsley, or cheese or onion to the sauce. Any 'vegetables-in-sauce' dish is enhanced by a crumble topping—see Seasonal Vegetables in Savoury Sauce, page 49.)

2.

Imperial (Metric)	American
1 large onion, diced	1 large onion, diced
½-1 lb (¼-1 kilo) courgettes, marrow or aubergines, roughly diced or sliced	½-1 lb zucchini, summer squash or eggplants, roughly diced or sliced
½ lb (¼ kilo) mushrooms, sliced	4 cupsful mushrooms, sliced
½ lb (¼ kilo) tomatoes, roughly diced	1¼ cupsful tomatoes, roughly diced
2 tablespoonsful vegetable oil	2½ tablespoonsful vegetable oil
Pinch of sweet basil and oregano	Pinch of sweet basil and oregano
Sea salt and freshly ground black pepper	Sea salt and freshly ground black pepper

1. *Sauté* the onion in the oil, then add the courgettes, marrow or aubergine. Cook for a few more minutes before adding the remaining ingredients.

2. Stir gently, cover the pan and leave to simmer for 5-10 minutes.

3. Pour the mixture into an ovenproof dish and cover with a crumble topping (page 47).

4. Bake at 350°F/180°C (Gas Mark 4) for about 20 minutes to brown the crumble.

3. Winter Stew (page 194) is also very good with a crumble topping.

Crumble Toppings:

1. Peanut Crumble

Imperial (Metric)	*American*
4 oz (100g) oats (rolled unpearled barley could sometimes be used instead)	1 cupful oats (rolled unpearled barley could sometimes be used instead)
2 oz (50g) wholemeal flour	½ cupful wholemeal flour
3 oz (75g) butter or vegetable oil	⅓ cupful butter or vegetable oil
2-3 oz (50-75g) peanuts	½-¾ cupful peanuts
Seasoning to taste	Seasoning to taste

1. Mix the ingredients together, adding the fat last and working it in well. Bake in the oven until the top is brown. (Soak the oats beforehand for a chewy consistency.)

2. Chick Pea Crumble
Use the recipe for Chick Pea Roast (page 38). Sprinkle the mixture over the vegetables and brown the crumble in the oven.

3. Lentil Crumble
Use the recipe for Lentil Roast (page 179) and proceed as for Chick Pea Crumble (above).

4. Bran Crumble

Imperial (Metric)	*American*
1-2 oz (25-50g) bran	¾-1½ cupful bran
1-2 oz (25-50g) wheat germ	¾-1½ cupful wheat germ
2 oz (50g) wholemeal flour	½ cupful wholemeal flour
2 oz (50g) butter	¼ cupful butter

1. Rub the butter into the flour, then add the other ingredients. Season to taste and add herbs to complement the flavour of the dish if you wish.

2. Bake at 350°F/180°C (Gas Mark 4) for about 20 minutes to brown the crumble topping.

5. Onion or Garlic Crumble

Imperial (Metric)	*American*
4 oz (100g) soft wholemeal breadcrumbs	2½ cupsful soft wholemeal breadcrumbs
1-2 oz (25-50g) melted butter or vegetable oil	2½-5 tablespoonsful melted butter or vegetable oil
1 onion, finely diced or	1 onion, finely diced or
1 clove garlic, crushed	1 clove garlic, crushed

1. Combine the ingredients thoroughly. Proceed as for Bran Crumble above.

6. Wheat Germ and Cheese Crumble

Imperial (Metric)	American
2 tablespoonsful each wheat germ and hard cheese, grated	2½ tablespoonsful each wheat germ and hard cheese, grated
1 tablespoonful seeds	1 tablespoonful seeds

1. Proceed as for Onion or Garlic Crumble (page 47).

7. Cottage Cheese Crumble

Imperial (Metric)	American
3 tablespoonsful fresh wholemeal breadcrumbs	4 tablespoonsful fresh wholemeal breadcrumbs
2 tablespoonsful cottage cheese	2½ tablespoonsful cottage cheese
2 tablespoonsful hazelnuts or walnuts, chopped	2½ tablespoonsful hazelnuts or walnuts, chopped

1. Proceed as for Onion or Garlic Crumble (page 47).

SAVOURY HARICOT PIE

Imperial (Metric)	American
4 oz (100g) haricot beans, soaked overnight	½ cupful navy beans, soaked overnight
2 onions, sliced finely into rings	2 onions, sliced finely into rings
2 oz (50g) butter or	¼ cupful butter or
2 tablespoonsful vegetable oil	2½ tablespoonsful vegetable oil
6 oz (200g) grated cheese	2 cupsful grated cheese
1 lb (½ kilo) potatoes, boiled and mashed with butter and milk or 1 egg	1 lb potatoes, boiled and mashed with butter and milk or 1 egg
¼ pint (150ml) boiling water	¾ cupful boiling water
1 level teaspoonful yeast extract	1 level teaspoonful yeast extract

1. Cook the beans, boiling them for 10 minutes and then simmering them for about 1½ hours.

2. *Sauté* the onions gently in the fat for about 20 minutes.

3. In a greased ovenproof dish, make two layers each of beans, onions and cheese. Pour over the yeast extract dissolved in the water.

4. Spread the potatoes over the layered mixture and bake in a moderate oven at 350°F/180°C (Gas Mark 4) for about 30 minutes.

SEASONAL VEGETABLES IN SAVOURY SAUCE

For this recipe, any fresh vegetables, very gently steamed until crisp and tender, may be used. Combinations of two or three vegetables are best. Occasionally, when fresh vegetables are difficult to vary, frozen vegetables such as broccoli, beans or sweet corn may be used to add flavour and texture. Rinse the frozen vegetables before adding them to the steamer for a few minutes.

Sauce:

Imperial (Metric)	American
1-2 oz (25-50g) butter or vegetable oil	2½-5 tablespoonful butter or vegetable oil
1-2 oz (25-50g) wholemeal flour	¼-½ cupful wholemeal flour
½-1 pint (¼-½ litre) liquid (½ cold, ½ tepid)	1¼-2½ cupful liquid (½ cold, ½ tepid)
—see below	—see below
Herbs to complement the vegetables used	Herbs to complement the vegetables used
Sea salt and freshly ground black pepper	Sea salt and freshly ground black pepper

1. Heat the fat, add the flour and mix well to make a paste. Cook for 1 minute then remove the pan from the heat.

2. Add the cold liquid, whisking well, then stir the liquid over a low heat, gradually adding the remaining liquid.

3. Add the seasonings and herbs and stir or whisk the sauce until it thickens and begins to coat the back of the spoon. (Do not overcook the sauce.)

4. Arrange the vegetables in an ovenproof dish and pour the sauce over the top. Sprinkle a crumble topping (page 47), some crunchy seeds, bran or wheat germ over the sauce and bake for about 20 minutes at 350°F/180°C (Gas Mark 4). Serve on its own or with a simple green salad.

Sauce Variations:

1. Use rice flour instead of wholewheat flour (100 per cent or 81 per cent).

2. Add any of the following flavourings to the milk or vegetable stock: *Marmite*, *Tastex* or *Vecon*; miso, tomato paste or mushroom essence; dry white wine.

3. To enrich the sauce, add any of the following:

    Yolk and/or white of 1 egg—beat the egg with 1 tablespoonful of the sauce before adding it to the rest of the sauce and stirring over a low heat;
    A little skimmed milk;
    Soured, single or double cream;
    4-6 oz (100-200g) grated cheese to 1 pint (½ litre) liquid;
    Plain yogurt may be used to thin down an over-thick sauce and add a piquant flavour.

SHEPHERD'S PIE

Imperial (Metric)	American
1 small packet tvp minced meat, hydrated	1 small packet tvp minced meat, hydrated
2 large onions, diced	2 large onions, diced
3 tablespoonsful vegetable oil	4 tablespoonsful vegetable oil
2 large carrots, grated	2 large carrots, grated
2 sticks celery, finely sliced	2 sticks celery, finely sliced
1 green pepper, diced	1 green pepper, diced
1 teaspoonful mixed herbs	1 teaspoonful mixed herbs
1 tablespoonful *Holbrook's* Worcester sauce	1 tablespoonful *Holbrook's* Worcester sauce
1 teaspoonful *Tastex* or *Vecon*	1 teaspoonful *Tastex* or *Vecon*
3 large potatoes, boiled and drained, reserving the water	3 large potatoes, boiled and drained, reserving the water
Sea salt and freshly ground black pepper	Sea salt and freshly ground black pepper

1. *Sauté* the onions in the oil and add the carrots, stirring well. Add the remaining ingredients and stir-fry for 10-15 minutes.

2. Place the mixture in an ovenproof pie dish and cover with the mashed potatoes, mixed with black pepper, sea salt, nutmeg, butter, chopped chives, onion or parsley, if liked. (A little of the cooking water may be added for a creamier texture.)

3. Brown the top under the grill or in a hot oven at 425°F/220°C (Gas Mark 7) for 10 minutes.

SLOW OMELETTE

Use the same mixture as for the Baked Omelette recipe (page 36) or simply use beaten eggs, increasing the quantity according to the number of people to be served.

1. *Sauté* the vegetables very gently in a large, heavy pan and then pour the omelette mixture over them, without stirring.

2. Allow the omelette to cook over a very low heat for about 10 minutes, covered for part of the time. When almost cooked, decorate the top and brown under the grill. Slice in large wedges to serve.

SPINACH AND BUCKWHEAT BAKE

Imperial (Metric)
1 lb (½ kilo) spinach
4 oz (100g) buckwheat
1 large onion, sliced
1 clove garlic, crushed
½ lb (¼ kilo) tomatoes, sliced thickly
Juice of half a lemon
Sea salt and freshly ground black pepper

American
1 lb spinach
½ cupful buckwheat
1 large onion, sliced
1 clove garlic, crushed
1¼ cupsful tomatoes, sliced thickly
Juice of half a lemon
Sea salt and freshly ground black pepper

1. *Sauté* the onion, garlic and buckwheat briefly.

2. Combine all the ingredients, cover with a tight-fitting lid and bake or simmer for half an hour, stirring and adding water or vegetable stock occasionally to keep it moist.

3. Serve with a mushroom sauce made with 4 oz (100g) mushrooms to ½ pint (¼ litre) white sauce (page 136).

SPINACH PANCAKES IN CHEESE SAUCE

Imperial (Metric)
2 lb (1 kilo) spinach
12 Pancake Omelettes (page 140)
1 pint (½ litre) cheese sauce (page 136)
Juice of half a lemon
Sea salt and freshly ground black pepper
Knob of butter
Extra grated cheese to garnish

American
2 lb spinach
12 Pancake Omelettes (page 140)
2½ cupsful cheese sauce (page 136)
Juice of half a lemon
Sea salt and freshly ground black pepper
Knob of butter
Extra grated cheese to garnish

1. Shred the spinach and cook it in the lemon juice, butter and seasoning.

2. Drain the spinach thoroughly, roll it up in the pancakes and arrange them in a shallow, buttered ovenproof dish.

3. Pour the sauce over the top, garnish with cheese and brown in a moderate oven at 350°F/180°C (Gas Mark 4) for 20-30 minutes. Serve the pancakes on their own or with a simple green salad and lemon juice dressing (page 128).

VEGETABLE SAUCE I

This sauce needs careful and thorough cooking with much stirring. It should be thick and very savoury, and may be served with spaghetti, noodles or lasagne.

Imperial (Metric)
2 sticks celery, diced
2 carrots, diced
1 pepper, diced
1 lb (½ kilo) tomatoes, chopped
½ lb (¼ kilo) mushrooms, sliced
2 onions, diced
1 clove garlic, crushed
2 tablespoonful tomato paste (optional)
2 tablespoonful red wine
2-3 tablespoonsful vegetable oil
Italian seasoning to taste
Sea salt and freshly ground black pepper

American
2 sticks celery, diced
2 carrots, diced
1 pepper, diced
1 lb tomatoes, chopped
4 cupsful mushrooms, sliced
2 onions, diced
1 clove garlic, crushed
2½ tablespoonsful tomato paste (optional)
2½ tablespoonsful red wine
3 tablespoonsful vegetable oil
Italian seasoning to taste
Sea salt and freshly ground black pepper

1. *Sauté* the onions and garlic in the oil. Add the carrots and celery and brown well.

2. Gradually stir in the other vegetables, browning them gently.

3. Stir in the paste and wine, season and cover.

4. Cook for 30 minutes, adding vegetable stock or water as necessary before serving.

VEGETABLES AND NOODLES

Add 4-6 oz (100-200g) of cooked wholemeal noodles to the vegetable sauce (above). Simmer for 5-10 minutes and season to taste before serving, topped with grated Parmesan or Cheddar cheese, dry roasted nuts and chopped parsley or sprigs of watercress.

Sweet Dishes

ALMOND-TOPPED APPLES

Imperial (Metric)	American
3-4 cooking apples, peeled and sliced	3-4 cooking apples, peeled and sliced
1-2 tablespoonsful honey	2 tablespoonsful honey
2 oz (50g) butter	¼ cupful butter
4 oz (100g) raw cane sugar	½ cupful raw cane sugar
2 eggs	2 eggs
4 oz (100g) ground almonds	1 cupful ground almonds
Rind of 1 lemon	Rind of 1 lemon
Water to cook the apples	Water to cook the apples

1. Simmer the apples until tender with a few tablespoonsful of water, the honey and lemon rind.

2. Cream the butter and sugar and then gradually beat in the eggs. Add the almonds and pour the mixture over the apples in an ovenproof dish.

3. Bake for 25-30 minutes or until the topping is golden at 350°F/180°C (Gas Mark 4).

APPLE AND MINT SALAD

Dice or slice the following unpeeled apples: 1 Granny Smith, 1 Cox's Orange Pippin or Golden Delicious and 1 Red Delicious. Add the chopped flesh of 1 large juicy orange or other citrus fruit and about 1 tablespoonful finely chopped fresh mint. Toss the ingredients well and decorate with sprigs of mint.

APPLE AND PINEAPPLE CRUMBLE

Imperial (Metric)
2 lb (1 kilo) Bramley apples, peeled, cored and cut into eighths
1 small tin pineapple pieces in its own juice
1 thick slice of lemon

American
2 lb Bramley apples, peeled, cored and cut into eighths
1 small tin pineapple pieces in its own juice
1 thick slice of lemon

1. Place the apples and lemon in a saucepan with very little water or a little pineapple juice.

2. Simmer until tender, remove the lemon and add the pineapple.

Crumble Topping

2 tablespoonsful of each of the following:

Desiccated coconut;
Ground almonds;
Wheatgerm;
Bran;
Sesame seeds;
Sunflower seeds;
Sunflower seed oil;
1 tablespoonful raw cane sugar (optional).

1. Combine the crumble ingredients thoroughly so that the oil is very well mixed.

2. Place the fruit in a shallow ovenproof dish. Sprinkle the crumble over the top and bake at 350°F/180°C (Gas Mark 4) until golden brown.

Note: Large quantities of the crumble mixture may be prepared and stored in air-tight containers in the refrigerator. Chopped nuts may be added to the crumble mixture and this goes equally well with other fruits (e.g. rhubarb stewed with a little ginger, banana halves placed in a well buttered dish and sprinkled with fruit juice before adding the crumble. Blackberries may be used to replace the pineapple in the autumn).

AVOCADO AND LIME DELIGHT

Imperial (Metric)
2 large, ripe smooth-skinned avocados
3 tablespoonsful raw cane sugar
2 tablespoonsful light honey
2-3 teaspoonsful agar-agar
¼ pint (150ml) double cream, whipped to form
  soft peaks
Juice of 3 large limes

American
2 large, ripe smooth-skinned avocados
4 tablespoonsful raw cane sugar
2½ tablespoonsful light honey
2-3 teaspoonsful agar-agar
1 cupful double cream, whipped to form soft
  peaks
Juice of 3 large limes

1. Measure out enough water to make up to ½ pint (¼ litre) with the lime juice, but keep the two separate.

2. Put the water in a saucepan with the agar-agar and stir it over a low heat to dissolve it.

3. Add the sugar or honey, stirring to dissolve it, then remove it from the heat and chill. When cool add the juice.

4. When the jelly is just about set, remove the flesh from the avocados and mash it until very smooth.

5. Combine the avocado with the jelly and fold in the cream.

6. Spoon the mixture into individual dishes and chill. Garnish with a sliver of lime dipped in raw cane sugar.

Note: Agar jellies never set in the same way as gelatine. They set quickly to a 'wobbly' consistency.

BANANA AND APPLE ZESTY SALAD

Slice and combine the following: 2 large ripe bananas, 1 red Delicious apple, 1 green eating apple, the zest of 1 or 2 lemons. Sprinkle with orange juice to moisten.

BANANA DELIGHTS

For each person peel and slice 1 ripe banana and sprinkle with lemon juice. Pour 1-2 table-spoonsful of double cream over each banana and top with coconut or raw cane sugar. This may be flashed under the grill until the sugar bubbles.

CHEESECAKE

Base:

Imperial (Metric)	American
3 oz (75g) butter	⅓ cupful butter
6 oz (200g) plain wholemeal flour	1½ cupsful plain wholemeal flour
1 egg yolk	1 egg yolk

1. Rub the butter into the flour and moisten with the egg yolk to make a firm dough. Line a 10 in. ovenproof pie dish.

Filling:

Imperial (Metric)	American
½ lb (¼ kilo) cottage cheese	1 cupful cottage cheese
½ lb (¼ kilo) cream cheese	1 cupful cream cheese
10 oz (300g) raw cane sugar	1¼ cupsful raw cane sugar
3 eggs, yolks and whites separated	3 eggs, yolks and whites separated
2 oz (50g) fresh wholemeal breadcrumbs	1⅓ cupsful fresh wholemeal breadcrumbs
Rind and juice of 1 lemon	Rind and juice of 1 lemon
Pure vanilla essence to taste	Pure vanilla essence to taste

1. Rub the cheeses together through a sieve. Mix in the sugar, vanilla, rind, juice and egg yolks.

2. Beat the egg whites until stiff, fold them into the cheese mixture and pour the filling into the case.

3. Sprinkle the top with breadcrumbs and bake for 30 minutes at 350°F/180°C (Gas Mark 4). (This cheesecake keeps well if wrapped in foil and stored in the refrigerator.)

COTTAGE CHEESE AND APPLE

Imperial (Metric)	American
1 lb (½ kilo) apples, sliced	1 lb apples, sliced
½ lemon, sliced	½ lemon, sliced
3-4 tablespoonsful water	4 tablespoonsful water
½ lb (¼ kilo) cottage cheese, sieved	1 cupful cottage cheese, sieved
1-2 tablespoonsful cream	2 tablespoonsful cream
½ teaspoonful cinnamon	½ teaspoonful cinnamon

1. Stew the apples gently with the lemon and water and, when cool, *purée* them in a blender or sieve them.

2. Add the remaining ingredients and blend thoroughly.

3. Pour the mixture into individual dishes, sprinkle with cinnamon and chill. (This dish has a refreshing sharpness.)

COTTAGE CHEESE TORTONI

Imperial (Metric)
½ lb (¼ kilo) cottage cheese
2 tablespoonsful double cream
½ lb (¼ kilo) crumbled ratafia biscuits
1-2 tablespoonsful sherry or brandy
½ teaspoonful cinnamon
A few toasted almonds

American
1 cupful cottage cheese
2½ tablespoonsful double cream
2½ cupsful crumbled ratafia biscuits
2 tablespoonsful sherry or brandy
½ teaspoonful cinnamon
A few toasted almonds

1. Combine the ingredients thoroughly, pour the mixture into individual dishes and garnish with cinnamon and toasted almonds before serving.

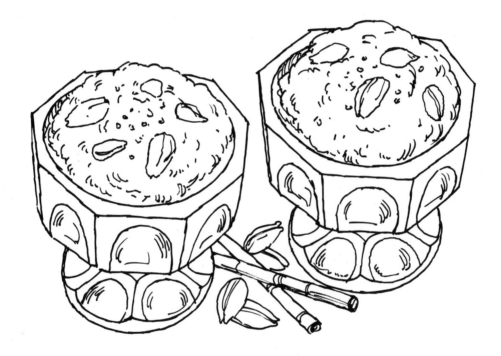

DRIED FRUIT IN WINE

Dried apricots or peaches in brandy;
Dried pears in green ginger wine;
Dried apples in damson or port wine.

Soak the fruit, 3-5 pieces per person, in hot water for 1 hour. Arrange the fruit in a shallow, covered dish. Cover with the brandy or wine according to the type of fruit used. Leave covered for at least 24 hours, preferably for 3-4 days, adding a little more liquid if necessary. The fruit may be served as it is or gently poached or *sautéed* and served with whipped cream.

FRUIT SHORTCAKE

Imperial (Metric)	American
3 oz (75g) butter	⅓ cupful butter
3 oz (75g) raw cane sugar	⅓ cupful raw cane sugar
1 egg yolk	1 egg yolk
6 oz (200g) plain wholemeal flour	1½ cupsful plain wholemeal flour
A quantity of stewed fruit (e.g. apples, berries or dried apricots)	A quantity of stewed fruit (e.g. apples, berries or dried apricots)

1. Cream the butter and sugar, beat in the egg yolk, then sift in the flour to make a firm dough. Set aside to chill for one hour.

2. Spread one half of the dough over the base of a baking tin lined with tin foil. Spread the fruit on the dough and cover this with the top layer of pastry.

3. Sprinkle with cinnamon and raw cane sugar (optional) and bake for 30 minutes at 350°F/180°C (Gas Mark 4). When cool, the top may be dredged with sugar.

4. Remove the shortcake from the tin using the tin foil and wrap it in greaseproof paper or clingfilm.

GRAPE FRUIT SALAD

(South African grapes are marvellous in England in the early spring.) For each person combine 2 oz (50g) each of black and white grapes, halved and seeded; 2 pears, sliced; 1 kiwi fruit, sliced.

GREEN AND GOLD FRUIT SALAD

Combine 2 kiwi fruit, sliced; ½ large pineapple, diced or 1 medium-sized tin diced pineapple in its own juice; 4 oz (100g) black grapes or diced mango.

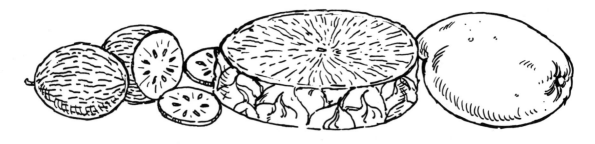

58

HONEYDEW SPICY SALAD

For each person cut a wedge of honeydew melon. Gently brush the surface with the juice of 1 lemon and 2 tablespoonsful of ginger syrup combined. Sprinkle with cinnamon. (Finely chopped crystallized ginger may also be sprinkled over the melon.)

NUT AND SEED MUESLI

Combine equal quantities of the following ingredients: Wheat germ; bran; coconut (freshly grated or desiccated); ground almonds; chopped nuts (peanuts are too strong); whole sesame seeds; whole or ground sunflower seeds; dried fruit, chopped or whole. Add 1-2 teaspoonsful of poppy or melon seeds (optional) and a good pinch of cinnamon or freshly grated nutmeg (optional). Store the muesli in an air-tight container in a cool, dry place.

ORANGE AND DATE SALAD

For each person combine 1 orange, chopped (the very dark orange, loose-skinned Israeli variety); chopped fresh or dried dates or figs. Sprinkle with grated fresh coconut.

PIKELETS

(Serves 2-3)

Imperial (Metric)
½ lb (¼ kilo) wholemeal flour (S.R.)
½ pint (¼ litre) milk
1 egg, beaten
1 tablespoonful raw cane sugar (optional)
1 tablespoonful poppy or sesame seeds
    (optional)
Butter for frying

American
2 cupsful wholemeal flour (S.R.)
1¼ cupsful milk
1 egg, beaten
1 tablespoonful raw cane sugar (optional)
1 tablespoonful poppy or sesame seeds
    (optional)
Butter for frying

1. Sift the dry ingredients together in a bowl and make a well in the centre.

2. Mix the beaten egg into the dry ingredients, gradually adding the milk to make a thick, satiny batter. Use a whisk to beat the mixture thoroughly.

3. Heat a heavy frying pan and drop in a little butter to grease the pan. When the butter begins to bubble, drop small tablespoonsful of the batter into the pan.

4. Cook the pikelets on both sides until golden. (Do not allow the pan to become too hot.) Serve the pikelets immediately in a large basket lined with a tea-towel to retain the heat.

RHUBARB FOOL

Imperial (Metric)
1 lb (½ kilo) rhubarb, cut into 1 in. pieces
1 teaspoonful ground or fresh root ginger,
  chopped
2-3 eggs
2 tablespoonful raw cane sugar or honey
¾ pint (400ml) milk
Few drops of pure vanilla essence
Grated rind of 1 lemon
Crystallized ginger to taste

American
1 lb rhubarb, cut into 1 in. pieces
1 teaspoonful ground or fresh root ginger,
  chopped
2-3 eggs
2½ tablespoonful raw cane sugar or honey
1¾ cupsful milk
Few drops of pure vanilla essence
Grated rind of 1 lemon
Crystallized ginger to taste

1. Heat the rhubarb gently with the ground or root ginger and lemon rind until tender.

2. Add the chopped crystallized ginger and chill.

3. Beat together the eggs and sugar or honey until thick and fluffy.

4. Meanwhile, heat the milk just to boiling point and pour a little of it onto the eggs. Beat well and gradually add all of the milk.

5. Return to a gentle heat and stir constantly with a wooden spoon until the custard mixture thickens.

6. Add the vanilla essence, allow to cool and combine the two mixtures.

7. Pour the dessert into tall glasses and chill. A little whipped or double cream may be used as a garnish.

Note: If a firm consistency is desired, sprinkle 1-2 tablespoonful of agar-agar into the hot fruit. Stir well and combine with the custard mixture as soon as possible.

SILESIAN PANCAKES

Imperial (Metric)
2 oz (50g) butter
2 tablespoonsful honey
2 eggs
2 oz (50g) wholemeal flour, sifted
¼ pint (150ml) yogurt
¼ pint (150ml) milk, slightly warmed

American
¼ cupful butter
2½ tablespoonsful honey
2 eggs
½ cupful wholemeal flour, sifted
⅔ cupful yogurt
⅔ cupful milk, slightly warmed

1. Cream the butter and honey. Add the eggs separately, beating well.

2. Fold in the flour and mix in the yogurt and milk.

3. Half fill greased patty tins with the mixture and bake at 350°F/180°C (Gas Mark 4) for 15 minutes. Serve warm.

SUMMER

Menu Suggestions

1.
Breakfast
Fresh pineapple
Boiled egg with wholewheat crispbread

Lunch
Watercress and Citrus Fruit Salad (p. 86) with yogurt (p. 112)

Dinner
Spanish Onion Soup (p. 80)
Courgettes Au Gratin (p. 87)

2.
Breakfast
Fresh cherries with yogurt (p. 112)
Prof. Shears' Muesli (p. 110)

Lunch
Cream of Asparagus Soup (p. 72)
Hot and Cold Salad (p. 84)
Cheese board or wholemeal bread

Dinner
Ratatouille (p. 98)
Green Platter (p. 83)
Fresh wholemeal bread and butter
Strawberries and cream

3.
Breakfast
Tomatoes and watercress on wholemeal toast

Lunch
Pepper, Avocado and Herb Salad (p. 84) with cottage cheese

Dinner
Aubergine and Pepper Pasta (p. 88)
Green salad
Compote of cherries and raspberries

4.
Breakfast
Yogurt (p. 112), wheatgerm and honey with seeds and fresh fruit

Lunch
Stuffed Tomato Salad (p. 85)
Apple, raisins and almonds

Dinner
French Beans and New Potatoes in Lemon Chive Sauce (p. 89)
Cottage Cheese and Peaches (p. 105)

5.
Breakfast
Apple, scrambled egg on wholemeal toast

Lunch
Broad Bean Salad (p. 81) with new potatoes

Dinner
Stuffed Marrow (p. 99) with steamed fresh vegetables
Jerusalem Artichokes au Gratin (p. 95)
Raspberry Mousse (p. 108)

6.
Breakfast
Sweet Toasted Oat Snack (p. 112) with fresh nectarines

Lunch
Cauliflower Salad (p. 81) with cheese

Dinner
Cream of Avocado Soup (p. 72)
or
Avocado and Tomato Entrée (p. 71)
Broccoli in Tomato Sauce (p. 90)

7.
Breakfast
Cherries, muesli or yogurt (pp. 110 and 112)

Lunch
Green Platter (p. 83)
Stuffed Eggs (p. 80)

Dinner
Wheat and Tomato Loaf (p. 102)
Savoury Pumpkin Fritters (p. 98) with green peas or beans
Apple Snow (p. 104)

8.
Breakfast
Raspberries and yogurt (p. 112)
Scrambled eggs

Lunch
Egg Pie (p. 94)
Tomato and Mint Salad (p. 85)

Dinner
Gazpacho (p. 73)
Green Peas and Rice in Cream Sauce (p. 94)

9.
Breakfast
Banana and grapefruit

Lunch
French beans tossed in oil and lemon dressing (p. 84)
Savoury Pots of Cheese (p. 76) with wholemeal bread

Dinner
Stuffed Peppers with Eggs (p. 100)
Courgette Casserole (p. 93) with brown rice or new potatoes

10.
Breakfast
Pineapple and orange
Cottage cheese on wholemeal toast

Lunch
Green and Red Salad (p. 82)
Cheese board with crispbread

Dinner
Lentil Croquettes (p. 96)
Tomato and Onion Pie (p. 101) with green beans or Courgette Casserole (p. 93)
Bread and Butter Plums (p. 104)

11.
Breakfast
Apple, raisins and almonds

Lunch
Cucumber and Pineapple Salad (p. 82) with cream cheese

Dinner
Cool Cucumber Soup (p. 71)
Cauliflower and Tomato Crumble with Hazelnuts (p. 91)
Fresh Fruit Salad (p. 106)

12.
Breakfast
Fresh strawberries and yogurt (p. 112)

Lunch
Stuffed Tomato Salad (p. 85)
Green Pea Salad (p. 83)
Carrot Cake (p. 104)

Dinner
Stuffed Marrow (p. 99)
Green Platter (p. 83)
or
Green Salad Galore (p. 83)

13.
Breakfast
Peach, poached egg on wholemeal toast
or
Sweet Toasted Oat Snack (p. 112)

Lunch
Hot and Cold Salad (p. 84)
Egg and Cheese Spread (p. 73) on wholemeal toast

Dinner
Glazed Carrots and Asparagus (p. 74)
Vegetable Soufflé (p. 102) with new potatoes
Exotic Fruit Salad (p. 106)

14.
Breakfast
Pineapple and banana with yogurt (p. 112)

Lunch
Green Pea Soup (p. 74)
Cheese Flan (p. 92)

Dinner
Tomatoes and Carrots (p. 101)
or
Courgette Casserole (p. 93) served in individual pots
Marrow with Parsley Stuffing (p. 96) with fresh green vegetables
Strawberry Mousse (p. 108)

Starters

AVOCADO AND TOMATO ENTRÉE

Imperial (Metric)
2 avocados
2 small tomatoes
2 tablespoonsful oil and cider vinegar
  dressing (page 30)

American
2 avocados
2 small tomatoes
2½ tablespoonsful oil and cider vinegar
  dressing (page 30)

1. Halve the avocados and remove the stones. Spoon chopped tomato into each seed groove
    and sprinkle the dressing over the top. (A small crushed clove of garlic may be added if
    liked.)

COOL CUCUMBER SOUP

Imperial (Metric)
2 large cucumbers, coarsely grated
1 pint (½ litre) natural yogurt
1-2 cloves garlic, finely crushed
1 tablespoonful mint, finely chopped
Juice of 2-3 lemons
Grated rind of 1 lemon

American
2 large cucumbers, coarsely grated
2½ cupsful natural yogurt
1-2 cloves garlic, finely crushed
1 tablespoonful mint, finely chopped
Juice of 2-3 lemons
Grated rind of 1 lemon

1. Combine all the ingredients.

2. Pour the soup into individual dishes and float a slice of cucumber, lemon or a sprig of mint
    to garnish.

Note: 1 dessertspoonful of double cream may be added to each bowl of soup before
garnishing.

CREAM OF ASPARAGUS SOUP

Imperial (Metric)
1-1½ lb (½-¾ kilo) asparagus
2 oz (50g) butter
2 oz (50g) wholemeal flour
½ pint (¼ litre) milk
1 tablespoonful Parmesan, farmhouse Cheddar
   or Gruyère cheese, finely grated
Pinch of nutmeg, freshly grated
¼ pint (150ml) single or double cream
   (optional)
Sea salt and freshly ground black pepper

American
1-1½ lb asparagus
¼ cupful butter
½ cupful wholemeal flour
1¼ cupsful milk
1 tablespoonful Parmesan, farmhouse Cheddar
   or Gruyère cheese, finely grated
Pinch of nutmeg, freshly grated
¾ cupful single or double cream
   (optional)
Sea salt and freshly ground black pepper

1. Trim the asparagus and stand it upright in a deep saucepan. Pour boiling water to half way up the stems and add about 1 tablespoonful of milk to the water. Simmer until tender, drain the asparagus and reserve the cooking water.

2. Meanwhile, prepare a roux with the butter and flour. Cook for 1 minute.

3. Remove the pan from the heat and add the milk. Stir constantly and return the pan to a low heat as the sauce begins to thicken.

4. Add ½ pint (¼ litre) of the asparagus stock and continue cooking. Gently chop the asparagus flesh, reserving the very tender tips and discarding any woody parts.

5. Add the flesh to the stock and sprinkle in the cheese. Season to taste.

6. Reheat but do not allow the soup to boil. Fill individual bowls with the soup and add the asparagus tips and cream to garnish.

Note: This soup may be served hot or cold. If cold, chill well in the refrigerator and place the bowls on a bed of crushed ice.

CREAM OF AVOCADO SOUP

Imperial (Metric)
2 large ripe avocado pears
1-1½ pints (½-¾ litre) vegetable stock
1 clove garlic, crushed
½ pint (¼ litre) single cream
Pinch of nutmeg, freshly grated
Sea salt and freshly ground black pepper

American
2 large ripe avocado pears
2½-3¾ cupsful vegetable stock
1 clove garlic, crushed
1¼ cupsful single cream
Pinch of nutmeg, freshly grated
Sea salt and freshly ground black pepper

1. Gently simmer the garlic in the stock.

2. Meanwhile, mash the avocados and add them to the stock immediately. Heat gently and pass the soup through a sieve or liquidize it to remove any lumps.

3. Add most of the cream, reserving about 1 dessertspoonful for each serving.

4. Simmer the soup briefly and season to taste.

5. Pour the soup into warm bowls and stir a little cream into each one. Sprinkle with the nutmeg to garnish.

Variation
Chill the avocado stock mixture. Fold in the single cream or a little whipped double cream. Serve in chilled bowls garnished with a slice of lemon on the side of each bowl.

EGG AND CHEESE SPREAD

Imperial (Metric)
2 hard-boiled eggs, chopped
4 oz (100g) cottage cheese
1 teaspoonful lemon rind
1 teaspoonful mustard
1 tablespoonful mayonnaise or oil and vinegar
   dressing (page 30)

American
2 hard-boiled eggs, chopped
½ cupful cottage cheese
1 teaspoonful lemon rind
1 teaspoonful mustard
1 tablespoonful mayonnaise or oil and vinegar
   dressing (page 30)

1. Combine all the ingredients and leave the spread in the fridge to chill. Serve on wholemeal bread with green salad, including plenty of watercress.

GAZPACHO

Imperial (Metric)
¾ lb (350g) ripe tomatoes
1 small cucumber
1 small onion
½ green pepper
2 sticks celery
1 clove garlic
¾ pint (400ml) tomato juice
2½ tablespoonful vegetable oil
1½ tablespoonful cider vinegar
Few drops of *Tabasco* sauce
Sea salt and freshly ground black pepper

American
¾ lb ripe tomatoes
1 small cucumber
1 small onion
½ green pepper
2 sticks celery
1 clove garlic
1¾ cupful tomato juice
3 tablespoonful vegetable oil
2 tablespoonful cider vinegar
Few drops of *Tabasco* sauce
Sea salt and freshly ground black pepper

1. Peel and coarsely dice the vegetables, reserving a small amount for garnish.

2. Blend or briefly liquidize the remaining vegetables and other ingredients.

3. Refrigerate for an hour or two and serve topped with the vegetable garnish.

Note: This makes an ideal starter for a 'special occasion' meal.

GLAZED CARROTS AND ASPARAGUS

1. Steam or quickly boil young whole carrots in a little water.

2. Cook the asparagus separately in boiling water with a little butter, or use canned asparagus if necessary.

3. Drain the vegetables carefully, arrange them in a buttered ovenproof dish and season them to taste. Dot liberally with butter and cover the dish.

4. Warm through gently to melt the butter and sprinkle a little lemon juice over the top before serving. (This dish deserves to be eaten alone and at leisure.)

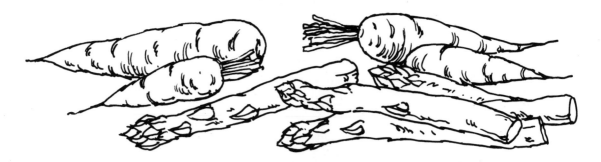

GREEN PEA SOUP

Imperial (Metric)	American
2 lb (1 kilo) fresh peas, shelled	2 lb fresh peas, shelled
2 tablespoonsful parsley, freshly chopped	2½ tablespoonsful parsley, freshly chopped
1 tablespoonful mint, finely chopped	1 tablespoonful mint, finely chopped
2 pints (1 litre) fresh vegetable stock	5 cupsful fresh vegetable stock
1 oz (25g) butter	2½ tablespoonsful butter
1 oz (25g) wholemeal flour	¼ cupful wholemeal flour
¼ pint (150ml) cream	¾ cupful cream
Sea salt and freshly ground black pepper	Sea salt and freshly ground black pepper

1. Simmer the peas and herbs together in the stock. When tender, strain them and reserve the stock.

2. Divide the peas and *purée* one half.

3. Melt the butter and cook the flour in it for 1 minute.

4. Gradually add the stock and the *purée*. Season to taste and add the cream and whole peas. Serve hot or cold.

Variation
Purée all the peas and add very small cooked carrots or new potatoes.

SUMMER

Cucumber and Apple Salad (page 82)
Tomato and Mushroom Salad (page 85)
Egg Pie (page 94)
Strawberry Mousse (page 108)

SAVOURY POTS OF CHEESE

In the following recipes, cottage cheese is served in small pots and dishes—ceramics, pottery, stoneware or pure china—amidst platters of the following:

1. *Crudités* such as tomato wedges, celery sticks, cucumber rounds, whole button mushrooms, red, yellow and green pepper slices, avocado slices dipped in lemon juice, apple rings, carrot sticks, cauliflower florets, gently steamed broad beans or mange-tout peas, lettuce, chicory, endive or young spinach leaves.

2. Fresh breads such as French sticks, wholemeal and granary buns or rolls, fancy loaves, rye bread, pumpernickel, French toasts.

3. Savoury crackers and crispbreads.

4. Popadams and potato crisps.

Each savoury pot of cheese uses 4 oz (100g) cottage cheese as its basis. The cheese may be left in its curd-textured state or sieved to give it a smooth texture. This is a very simple dish; mix the cottage cheese with any of the variations listed below. (All the quantities given are approximate—change the proportions to suit your own palate. Always check the carton before adding salt, as bought cheese is often already salted.)

Imperial (Metric)	*American*
1.	
2 oz (50g) lactic cheese, sieved	¼ cupful lactic cheese, sieved
1 small clove garlic, crushed	1 small clove garlic, crushed
½-1 teaspoonful Meaux mustard	½-1 teaspoonful Meaux mustard
1 dessertspoonful brandy	1 tablespoonful brandy
Few drops of lemon juice	Few drops of lemon juice
Lemon peel or mustard to garnish	Lemon peel or mustard to garnish
2.	
2 oz (50g) Cheddar cheese, finely grated	⅓ cupful Cheddar cheese, finely grated
1 heaped teaspoonful *Urchfont Mild Honey* mustard	1 heaped teaspoonful *Urchfont Mild Honey* mustard
Generous dash of freshly ground black pepper	Generous dash of freshly ground black pepper
Grated Cheddar cheese to garnish	Grated Cheddar cheese to garnish
3.	
1 small onion, finely diced	1 small onion, finely diced
½ teaspoonful dried sage	½ teaspoonful dried sage
Diced onion and sage to garnish	Diced onion and sage to garnish
4.	
½ teaspoonful tomato paste	½ teaspoonful tomato paste
1 small clove garlic, crushed (optional)	1 small clove garlic, crushed (optional)
Generous pinch of rosemary and basil	Generous pinch of rosemary and basil
Fresh lemon juice to taste	Fresh lemon juice to taste
Sprigs of fresh herbs to garnish	Sprigs of fresh herbs to garnish

5.

1 tablespoonful natural yogurt
2-3 tablespoonsful cucumber, grated
1 teaspoonful parsley, chopped (optional)
Freshly ground black pepper
Slivers of cucumber to garnish

1 tablespoonful natural yogurt
3 tablespoonsful cucumber, grated
1 teaspoonful parsley, chopped (optional)
Freshly ground black pepper
Slivers of cucumber to garnish

6.

2 tablespoonsful natural yogurt
Mint sauce to taste (preferably home-made)
Sprigs of fresh mint to garnish

2½ tablespoonsful natural yogurt
Mint sauce to taste (preferably home-made)
Sprigs of fresh mint to garnish

7.

1-2 tablespoonsful fresh chives, chopped
Dash of freshly ground black pepper
Chopped chives to garnish

1-2 tablespoonsful fresh chives, chopped
Dash of freshly ground black pepper
Chopped chives to garnish

8.

½ teaspoonful *Marmite* or *Tastex*
1 dessertspoonful onion, chives or parsley,
    chopped (optional) or
Mushrooms, finely chopped (optional)
Herbs or chopped walnuts to garnish

½ teaspoonful *Marmite* or *Tastex*
1 tablespoonful onion, chives or parsley,
    chopped (optional) or
Mushrooms, finely chopped (optional)
Herbs or chopped walnuts to garnish

9.

2 tablespoonsful natural yogurt
1 large clove garlic, crushed
1-2 allspice, crushed or a sprinkling to taste
Generous dash of freshly ground black pepper
Whole peppercorns or allspice to garnish

2½ tablespoonsful natural yogurt
1 large clove garlic, crushed
1-2 allspice, crushed or a sprinkling to taste
Generous dash of freshly ground black pepper
Whole peppercorns or allspice to garnish

10.

½ teaspoonful fennel seeds (optional)
Dash each of soy sauce and *Holbrook's*
    Worcester sauce
Pinch each of ground cumin and coriander
Lemon juice to taste
Fennel seeds to garnish

½ teaspoonful fennel seeds (optional)
Dash each of soy sauce and *Holbrook's*
    Worcester sauce
Pinch each of ground cumin and coriander
Lemon juice to taste
Fennel seeds to garnish

11.

1-2 tablespoonsful soured cream
1 clove garlic, crushed
1 dessertspoonful fresh parsley, chopped
Sprig of fresh parsley to garnish

1-2 tablespoonsful soured cream
1 clove garlic, crushed
1 tablespoonful fresh parsley, chopped
Sprig of fresh parsley to garnish

12.

4 oz (100g) cream cheese	½ cupful cream cheese
2 tablespoonsful spring onions, chopped (optional)	2½ tablespoonsful spring onions, chopped (optional)
Generous dash of freshly grated nutmeg	Generous dash of freshly grated nutmeg
Spring onion or grated nutmeg to garnish	Spring onion or grated nutmeg to garnish

13.

2 oz (50g) cream or lactic cheese	½ cupful cream or lactic cheese
½ teaspoonful curry powder	½ teaspoonful curry powder
½ teaspoonful garam masala	½ teaspoonful garam masala
Lemon juice to taste	Lemon juice to taste
Sprinkling of garam masala to garnish	Sprinkling of garam masala to garnish

14.

2 oz (50g) Stilton cheese, crumbled or finely diced	½ cupful Stilton cheese, crumbled or finely diced
Port wine to taste	Port wine to taste
Tiny strips of Stilton rind in a wheel shape to garnish	Tiny strips of Stilton rind in a wheel shape to garnish

15.

2 oz (50g) button mushrooms, sliced and *sautéed*	1 cupful button mushrooms, sliced and *sautéed*
Sprinkling of chopped fresh rosemary	Sprinkling of chopped fresh rosemary
Lemon juice to taste	Lemon juice to taste
1 whole mushroom, stalk trimmed, cup uppermost to garnish	1 whole mushroom, stalk trimmed, cup uppermost to garnish

16.

Approx. 1 tablespoonful Tilsit cheese, coarsely grated or diced	1 tablespoonful Tilsit cheese, coarsely grated or diced
1-2 teaspoonsful chives, chopped	1-2 teaspoonsful chives, chopped
Beer to moisten	Beer to moisten
Chives or grated cheese to garnish	Chives or grated cheese to garnish

17.

1 oz (25g) fresh Parmesan cheese, finely grated	¼ cupful fresh Parmesan cheese, finely grated
¼ teaspoonful dried basil or	¼ teaspoonful dried basil or
½ teaspoonful fresh basil, chopped	½ teaspoonful fresh basil, chopped
¼ teaspoonful tomato paste	¼ teaspoonful tomato paste
Sprig of fresh basil to garnish	Sprig of fresh basil to garnish

18.

1 tablespoonful freshly chopped walnuts	1 tablespoonful freshly chopped walnuts
1 tablespoonful farmhouse Cheddar cheese, coarsely grated	1 tablespoonful farmhouse Cheddar cheese, coarsely grated
Whole walnuts to garnish	Whole walnuts to garnish

SUMMER

Ratatouille (page 98)
Watercress and Citrus Fruit Salad (page 86)
Fresh Fruit Salad (page 106)

SPANISH ONION SOUP

Imperial (Metric)
2 large sweet Spanish onions
1-2 large cloves garlic, crushed
2 tablespoonsful olive oil
1 lb (½ kilo) tomatoes, skinned and chopped
½ lb (¼ kilo) sliced courgettes or fresh green peas or beans
1 large potato, chopped or
1 tablespoonful brown rice or
1 oz (25g) wholemeal pasta
1 teaspoonful basil
1 teaspoonful rosemary
2 teaspoonsful ground pimento
2 pints (1 litre) vegetable stock

American
2 large sweet Spanish onions
1-2 large cloves garlic, crushed
2½ tablespoonsful olive oil
1 lb tomatoes, skinned and chopped
2 cupsful sliced zucchini or fresh green peas or beans
1 large potato, chopped or
1 tablespoonful brown rice or
¼ cupful wholemeal pasta
1 teaspoonful basil
1 teaspoonful rosemary
2 teaspoonsful ground pimento
5 cupsful vegetable stock

1. Peel the onions, keeping a little of the best skin to brown the stock. Chop one onion finely and slice the other into rings.

2. Soften the onion and garlic in the oil over a low heat.

3. Add the potato and courgettes, if used, stir in the pimento and the tomatoes and simmer gently for 10-15 minutes.

4. Add the herbs and stock. (If using rice, add this before covering the pot and simmering the soup for 30-40 minutes. If using peas or beans and pasta, add them 20 minutes before serving.)

5. Remove the onion peel before serving with crusty wholemeal bread and butter.

STUFFED EGGS

Take 1 hard-boiled egg per person. Halve the eggs and scoop out the yolks. Mix the egg yolks thoroughly with the following ingredients:

Sea salt and freshly ground black pepper;
A pinch each of curry powder and mustard;
Or tomato paste to taste;
A dash of milk or cream.

Beat the mixture until it is fluffy and then fill the egg whites. Garnish with sprigs of parsley, mint or slivers of pepper—red or green.

Salads and Salad Dressings

BROAD BEAN SALAD

Imperial (Metric)
1½ lb (¾ kilo) broad beans, depodded and
  steamed
½ lb (¼ kilo) button mushrooms, sliced
½ medium-sized onion, diced finely
Freshly grated nutmeg

American
4 cupsful broad beans, depodded and
  steamed
4 cupsful button mushrooms, sliced
½ medium-sized onion, diced finely
Freshly grated nutmeg

1. While the beans are still warm, combine all the ingredients.

2. Toss the salad in a dressing of your choice and leave to cool in a covered bowl or chill.

CAULIFLOWER SALAD

Imperial (Metric)
1 small cauliflower, separated into florets
4 oz (100g) button mushrooms, sliced
½ lb (¼ kilo) tomatoes, cut into wedges
1 apple, sliced
½ small onion, diced (optional)

American
1 small cauliflower, separated into florets
4 oz (100g) button mushrooms, sliced
1¼ cupsful tomatoes, cut into wedges
1 apple, sliced
½ small onion, diced (optional)

1. Toss all the salad ingredients in an oil and vinegar dressing (page 30) with a little basil.

CUCUMBER AND APPLE SALAD

Imperial (Metric)
1 large cucumber, diced
2 large apples—1 green, 1 red, cut into wedges
1 small carton yogurt
Pinch of cinnamon

American
1 large cucumber, diced
2 large apples—1 green, 1 red, cut into wedges
1 small carton yogurt
Pinch of cinnamon

1.   Combine the ingredients, coating the cucumber and apple thoroughly with the yogurt.

2.   Sprinkle sparsely with cinnamon before serving.

CUCUMBER AND PINEAPPLE SALAD

Imperial (Metric)
1 cucumber, sliced
1 small pineapple, peeled, sliced and cut into
   wedges
2 oz (50g) almonds, blanched and halved
Juice of 1 lemon

American
1 cucumber, sliced
1 small pineapple, peeled, sliced and cut into
   wedges
½ cupful almonds, blanched and halved
Juice of 1 lemon

1.   Combine all the ingredients and serve.

GREEN AND RED SALAD

Imperial (Metric)
1 lb (½ kilo) French beans, sliced and steamed
¾ lb (350g) tomatoes, cut into small wedges
1 small red pepper, sliced
1 small green pepper, sliced
1 small onion, sliced into rings

American
1 lb French beans, sliced and steamed
¾ lb tomatoes, cut into small wedges
1 small red pepper, sliced
1 small green pepper, sliced
1 small onion, sliced into rings

1.   Combine all the ingredients while the beans are still warm.

2.   Toss the salad in a French dressing (page 171), cover and leave to cool.

GREEN PEA SALAD

Imperial (Metric)
1½ lb (¾ kilo) fresh young green peas,
    depodded and steamed
4 oz (100g) button mushrooms, sliced
2-3 sticks celery, sliced
1 small clove garlic, crushed finely

American
1½ lb fresh young green peas, depodded and
    steamed
2 cupsful button mushrooms, sliced
2-3 sticks celery, sliced
1 small clove garlic, crushed finely

1. Combine all the ingredients while the peas are still warm and toss them in an oil and vinegar or French dressing (pages 30 and 171). Cover and leave to cool.

GREEN PLATTER

Imperial (Metric)
1 avocado, peeled finely and sliced
2 tablespoonsful green olives
1 bunch asparagus
4-6 small artichoke hearts

American
1 avocado, peeled finely and sliced
2½ tablespoonsful green olives
1 bunch asparagus
4-6 small artichoke hearts

1. Simmer the asparagus, stalk ends down, in a little water.

2. Combine all the ingredients and arrange them on a bed of cos lettuce.

GREEN SALAD GALORE
(A large salad, ideal for a buffet dinner)

Imperial (Metric)
1 bunch watercress
1 cos or density lettuce
1 bunch spring onions, sliced into rings
2 large green peppers, cut into rings
4 oz (100g) bean sprouts
½ medium-sized cauliflower
4 oz (100g) mushrooms, sliced or quartered

American
1 bunch watercress
1 cos or density lettuce
1 bunch spring onions, sliced into rings
2 large green peppers, cut into rings
2 cupsful bean sprouts
½ medium-sized cauliflower
2 cupsful mushrooms, sliced or quartered

1. Wash and prepare all the vegetables: separate the watercress into sprigs and chop the stalks finely. Tear the lettuce into bite-sized pieces and break the cauliflower into very small florets.

2. Toss the salad in a French dressing (page 171) just before serving.

HOT AND COLD SALAD

Imperial (Metric)
1 large bunch radishes, washed and sliced
1 large cucumber, diced
1 small carton soured cream
Juice of ½ lemon
Sea salt and freshly ground black pepper

American
1 large bunch radishes, washed and sliced
1 large cucumber, diced
1 small carton soured cream
Juice of ½ lemon
Sea salt and freshly ground black pepper

1. Combine all the ingredients thoroughly to coat the vegetables in the cream.

OIL AND LEMON DRESSING

Imperial (Metric)
3 tablespoonsful olive oil
1 tablespoonful lemon juice
Pinch of pimento and raw cane sugar
1 teaspoonful honey
1 teaspoonful French mustard
Sea salt and freshly ground black pepper

American
4 tablespoonsful olive oil
1 tablespoonful lemon juice
Pinch of pimento and raw cane sugar
1 teaspoonful honey
1 teaspoonful French mustard
Sea salt and freshly ground black pepper

1. Blend the ingredients thoroughly.

PEPPER, AVOCADO AND HERB SALAD

Imperial (Metric)
2 large peppers, 1 green, 1 red,
   sliced into rings
1 avocado, peeled and sliced, not too finely
4-5 spring onions, sliced
Approx. 1 oz (25g) fresh parsley, separated
   into sprigs
2 tablespoonsful fresh mint, chopped
Juice of 1 lemon
Sea salt and freshly ground black pepper

American
2 large peppers, 1 green, 1 red,
   sliced into rings
1 avocado, peeled and sliced, not too finely
4-5 spring onions, sliced
½ cupful fresh parsley, separated into
   sprigs
2½ tablespoonsful fresh mint, chopped
Juice of 1 lemon
Sea salt and freshly ground black pepper

1. Combine all the ingredients, using the fresh herbs to garnish. (On no account use dried herbs!)

STUFFED TOMATO SALAD

Imperial (Metric)
4-6 large, firm but ripe tomatoes
1 stick celery
1 green pepper, diced finely
¼ medium-sized onion, diced finely
1 avocado, peeled and diced
Slices of lemon to garnish

American
4-6 large, firm but ripe tomatoes
1 stick celery
1 green pepper, diced finely
¼ medium-sized onion, diced finely
1 avocado, peeled and diced
Slices of lemon to garnish

1. Combine all the ingredients, except the tomatoes with an oil and vinegar dressing (page 30). Allow the flavours to mingle.

2. Cut the tops off the tomatoes and scoop out the seeds and central flesh, leaving a firm cup. Either add the tomato flesh to the mixture or use it in a stock or a vegetable dish.

3. Stuff the tomatoes with the mixture and garnish each one with a slice of lemon.

TOMATO AND MINT SALAD

Imperial (Metric)
1 lb (½ kilo) tomatoes, sliced
1-2 tablespoonsful fresh mint, chopped
A few sprigs of mint to garnish
A little lemon juice

American
1 lb tomatoes, sliced
1-2 tablespoonsful fresh mint, chopped
A few sprigs of mint to garnish
A little lemon juice

1. Mix together the tomatoes and chopped mint, then sprinkle the lemon juice over the top and garnish with the mint sprigs.

TOMATO AND MUSHROOM SALAD

Imperial (Metric)
1 lb (½ kilo) tomatoes, cut into wedges
½ lb (¼ kilo) button mushrooms, halved or
   quartered
3 tablespoonsful chopped chives

American
1 lb tomatoes, cut into wedges
4 cupsful button mushrooms, halved or
   quartered
4 tablespoonsful chopped chives

1. Combine all the ingredients and mix in an oil and vinegar or French dressing (pages 30 and 171) with garlic or oregano.

TOMATO DRESSING

Imperial (Metric)	American
4 tablespoonsful sunflower seed oil	5 tablespoonsful sunflower seed oil
1-2 tablespoonsful cider vinegar	1-2 tablespoonsful cider vinegar
1 tablespoonful tomato paste	1 tablespoonful tomato paste
Pinch each of basil or rosemary and pimento	Pinch each of basil or rosemary and pimento
Drop of *Tabasco* sauce	Drop of *Tabasco* sauce
Sea salt and freshly ground black pepper	Sea salt and freshly ground black pepper

1.   Blend all the ingredients together thoroughly.

VINAIGRETTE

Imperial (Metric)	American
6 tablespoonsful vegetable oil	7½ tablespoonsful vegetable oil
2 tablespoonsful tarragon vinegar	2½ tablespoonsful tarragon vinegar
¼ teaspoonful dry mustard	¼ teaspoonful dry mustard
1 tablespoonful gherkin, parsley and capers, chopped	1 tablespoonful gherkin, parsley and capers, chopped
Pinch of raw cane sugar	Pinch of raw cane sugar
Sea salt and freshly ground black pepper	Sea salt and freshly ground black pepper

1.   Blend the ingredients together thoroughly. (This dressing is especially good when served with sliced mushrooms.)

WATERCRESS AND CITRUS FRUIT SALAD

1 bunch watercress, soaked in cold water, drained and separated into sprigs. Chop the stalks finely;
2 oranges or 1 orange and 1 grapefruit, peeled and cut between segments so that the bright flesh is to the surface;
Juice of 1 lemon or a salad dressing;
1 teaspoonful honey;
1 tablespoonful sunflower seed oil;
(Sliced cucumber may be added and 2 tablespoonsful chopped chives may replace the watercress.)

1.   Combine the ingredients thoroughly.

Savoury Dishes

AU GRATIN DISHES

A variety of bases may be used with this recipe. Choose about 1-2 lb (½-1 kilo) of vegetables in season, e.g. aubergines, cauliflower, broccoli, green beans, mushrooms, leeks, marrow, celery, potatoes and sweet corn. Steam the vegetables until tender but still crisp. Toss them in a little butter, place them in an ovenproof dish and keep them warm.

Sauce:

Imperial (Metric)	*American*
1 onion, diced finely	1 onion, diced finely
1 clove garlic, crushed	1 clove garlic, crushed
1-2 tablespoonsful vegetable oil	1-2 tablespoonsful vegetable oil
1 tablespoonful wholemeal flour	1 tablespoonful wholemeal flour
1 medium-sized tin tomatoes or	1 medium-sized tin tomatoes or
1 lb (½ kilo) fresh tomatoes, peeled and chopped	1 lb fresh tomatoes, peeled and chopped
4 oz (100g) Cheddar or Swiss cheese, grated	1⅓ cupful Cheddar or Swiss cheese, grated
Raw cane sugar to taste	Raw cane sugar to taste
Sea salt and freshly ground black pepper	Sea salt and freshly ground black pepper

1. *Sauté* the onion and garlic in the oil, add the flour and cook for a few minutes.

2. Add the tomatoes and stir well. Mix in the seasoning and a little dry sherry if liked.

3. Pour the sauce over the vegetables, top with grated cheese and brown under the grill or in the oven. (In winter, black-eyed or haricot beans (well cooked) may be used in a similar way.)

AUBERGINE AND PEPPER PASTA

Imperial (Metric)	American
1 large aubergine, peeled and cut into strips or slices	1 eggplant, peeled and cut into strips or slices
1 large green pepper, sliced finely	1 large green pepper, sliced finely
2 tablespoonsful olive oil	2½ tablespoonsful olive oil
1 large onion, diced	1 large onion, diced
2 cloves garlic, crushed	2 cloves garlic, crushed
6 oz (200g) dry tvp 'mince', reconstituted	1½ cupsful dry tvp 'mince', reconstituted
2 tablespoonsful vegetable oil	2½ tablespoonsful vegetable oil
1-2 tablespoonsful tomato paste	1-2 tablespoonsful tomato paste
Pinch of basil	Pinch of basil
4 oz (100g) raw wholemeal lasagne or other noodles, cooked	1 cupful raw wholemeal lasagne or other noodles, cooked
2 oz (50g) butter	¼ cupful butter
2 oz (50g) wholemeal flour	½ cupful wholemeal flour
½ pint (¼ litre) vegetable stock	1¼ cupsful vegetable stock
½ pint (¼ litre) milk	1¼ cupsful milk
2 oz (50g) cream cheese	¼ cupful cream cheese
1 teaspoonful *Vecon*	1 teaspoonful *Vecon*
2 tablespoonsful sunflower seeds	2½ tablespoonsful sunflower seeds
2 tablespoonsful grated cheese	2½ tablespoonsful grated cheese
Sea salt and freshly ground black pepper	Sea salt and freshly ground black pepper

1. Place the aubergine slices in a colander, sprinkle them with salt and weight them down with a heavy plate. Set them aside for ½ hour so that the bitter juices are released. Rinse and drain them well.

2. Meanwhile, heat the vegetable oil in a saucepan and *sauté* the onion and garlic. Stir in the tvp, tomato paste, basil and then season to taste.

3. Reduce the heat to very low and gently simmer the mixture, covered, for about 20 minutes.

4. Melt the butter, add the flour and cook for 1 minute. Remove the saucepan from the heat, add the stock and then stir constantly over a low heat.

5. Gradually add the milk and *Vecon* and when the sauce thickens stir in the cream cheese, whisking well to dissolve it.

6. Fry the aubergines on one side only using the olive oil. Drain them well.

7. Assemble the dish by placing the 'mince' and tomato sauce in a greased shallow ovenproof dish followed by the pasta and half of the white sauce. Top with the aubergines and uncooked peppers followed by the remaining sauce. Sprinkle the seeds and grated cheese over the top.

8. Bake for 30 minutes at 350°F/180°C (Gas Mark 4) to brown the top.

Variation
This dish could be varied by substituting cooked brown rice for the pasta, Vegetable Sauce I (page 52) instead of the tvp sauce, and mushroom-flavoured white sauce instead of *Vecon*.

BEANS AND NEW POTATOES IN LEMON CHIVE SAUCE

Imperial (Metric)
1 lb (½ kilo) new potatoes, scrubbed
1 lb (½ kilo) French beans, de-stringed and
   sliced
Pinch of nutmeg, freshly grated

American
1 lb new potatoes, scrubbed
1 lb string beans, de-stringed and
   sliced
Pinch of nutmeg, freshly grated

Sauce:

4 oz (100g) butter
3 tablespoonsful chives, finely chopped
Grated rind and juice of 1 lemon

½ cupful butter
4 tablespoonsful chives, finely chopped
Grated rind and juice of 1 lemon

1. Steam the vegetables separately.

2. Peel the potatoes and sprinkle a little nutmeg over them. Toss them lightly with the beans in a serving dish.

3. Combine all the sauce ingredients and heat the mixture in a small saucepan over a low heat.

4. Pour the sauce over the vegetables and toss them gently until well coated.

Note: Serve this dish on its own or with an omelette or nut loaf.

BROCCOLI IN TOMATO SAUCE

Imperial (Metric)
1 lb (½ kilo) broccoli, cut into florets and
   steamed
1 lb (½ kilo) ripe tomatoes, skinned and
   chopped
¼ pint (150ml) cider vinegar
2 cloves garlic, crushed
¼ teaspoonful ground ginger or
½ teaspoonful root ginger, finely chopped
1 teaspoonful raw cane sugar
Pinch of cayenne pepper
Freshly ground black pepper

American
1 lb broccoli, cut into florets and
   steamed
1 lb ripe tomatoes, skinned and
   chopped
¾ cupful cider vinegar
2 cloves garlic, crushed
¼ teaspoonful ground ginger or
½ teaspoonful root ginger, finely chopped
1 teaspoonful raw cane sugar
Pinch of cayenne pepper
Freshly ground black pepper

1. Combine all the ingredients except for the broccoli, and sieve or liquidize the mixture to make a smooth sauce.

2. Bake at 350°F/180°C (Gas Mark 4) for about 20-30 minutes in a covered casserole.

3. Place the broccoli on a serving dish and pour over the tomato sauce.

Note: Serve this dish accompanied by baked new potatoes tossed in butter and chopped parsley.

BUTTER BEANS AU GRATIN

Imperial (Metric)
½ lb (¼ kilo) butter beans, soaked and cooked
1 medium-sized tin tomatoes or
1 lb (½ kilo) fresh tomatoes, peeled and
   chopped
1 large onion, diced
1 clove garlic, crushed
2-3 tablespoonsful vegetable oil or butter
1 oz (25g) wholemeal flour
3 tablespoonsful fresh wholemeal breadcrumbs
3 tablespoonsful sunflower or sesame seeds
Pinch of sweet basil and rosemary
Vegetable stock as required
Sea salt and freshly ground black pepper

American
1 cupful navy beans, soaked and cooked
1 medium-sized tin tomatoes or
1 lb fresh tomatoes, peeled and
   chopped
1 large onion, diced
1 clove garlic, crushed
3 tablespoonsful vegetable oil or butter
¼ cupful wholemeal flour
4 tablespoonsful fresh wholemeal breadcrumbs
4 tablespoonsful sunflower or sesame seeds
Pinch of sweet basil and rosemary
Vegetable stock as required
Sea salt and freshly ground black pepper

1. *Sauté* the onion and garlic in the butter or oil, then stir in the flour, herbs and seasoning.

2. Cook for 2-3 minutes then add the tomatoes, stirring well to make a thick sauce. Add a little vegetable stock if necessary.

3. Place the beans in an oiled, ovenproof dish, pour the sauce over them and garnish with breadcrumbs and seeds. Bake for 30 minutes at 350°F/180°C (Gas Mark 4) to crisp the topping.

CAULIFLOWER AND NOODLE BAKE

Imperial (Metric)
2 oz (50g) fresh wholemeal breadcrumbs
2 oz (50g) grated cheese
1 medium-sized cauliflower divided into florets and gently steamed
½ lb (¼ kilo) egg noodles, cooked but still chewy
1 pint (½ litre) cheese sauce (page 136) with 1 beaten egg added
Pinch of rosemary or *fines herbes*
Freshly ground black pepper and cayenne pepper to taste

American
1¼ cupsful fresh wholemeal breadcrumbs
⅔ cupful grated cheese
1 medium-sized cauliflower divided into florets and gently steamed
½ lb egg noodles, cooked but still chewy
2½ cupsful cheese sauce (page 136) with 1 beaten egg added
Pinch of rosemary or *fines herbes*
Freshly ground black pepper and cayenne pepper to taste

1. Combine all the ingredients in an ovenproof dish and top with the breadcrumbs and grated cheese.

2. Bake for 20-30 minutes at 350°F/180°C (Gas Mark 4) to brown. Serve with a green salad.

CAULIFLOWER AND TOMATO CRUMBLE WITH HAZELNUTS

Imperial (Metric)
2 oz (50g) soft wholemeal breadcrumbs
4 oz (100g) red lentils, cooked and drained
4 oz (100g) hazelnuts, roughly ground
Herbs to taste
Sea salt and freshly ground black pepper

American
1¼ cupsful soft wholemeal breadcrumbs
½ cupful red lentils, cooked and drained
1 cupful hazelnuts, roughly ground
Herbs to taste
Sea salt and freshly ground black pepper

Vegetable Base:
Lightly steamed carrot sticks, cauliflower florets and whole mushrooms; tomato sauce (page 90) with a pinch of rosemary.

1. Layer half the vegetables, tomato sauce and crumble and repeat, finishing with crumble. Bake for 40 minutes at 350°F/180°C (Gas Mark 4).

CHEESE FLAN

Pastry:

Imperial (Metric)	*American*
6 oz (200g) wholemeal flour	1½ cupsful wholemeal flour
3 tablespoonsful butter or vegetable oil	4 tablespoonsful butter or vegetable oil
1 egg yolk, beaten	1 egg yolk, beaten

1. Rub the butter or oil into the sieved flour and mix to a firm pliable dough with the egg yolk and a small amount of cold water if necessary.

2. Line an 8 in. pie dish with the pastry and prick with a fork or cover it with a layer of tin foil.

3. Bake the pastry for 20 minutes at 400°F/200°C (Gas Mark 6). Set aside to cool a little before pouring the filling into the shell.

Filling:

Imperial (Metric)	*American*
6 oz (200g) grated cheese or	2 cupsful grated cheese or
3 oz (75g) each grated cheese and cottage cheese	1 cupful grated cheese and ⅓ cupful cottage cheese
2 eggs	2 eggs
1 tablespoonful yogurt	1 tablespoonful yogurt
⅓ pint (200ml) milk or milk and cream	1 cupful milk or milk and cream
Pinch of cayenne pepper and *fines herbes*	Pinch of cayenne pepper and *fines herbes*
Sea salt and freshly ground black pepper	Sea salt and freshly ground black pepper
Grated cheese, *sautéed* mushrooms or sesame seeds	Grated cheese, *sautéed* mushrooms or sesame seeds

1. Blend all but the last ingredients thoroughly and pour the mixture into the pastry case. Sprinkle the cheese, mushrooms or seeds over the top.

2. Bake at 300°F/150°C (Gas Mark 2) for about 30 minutes. Serve hot or cold. (This flan keeps well if covered with clingfilm or tin foil and stored in a cool place.)

Variations
Any of the following vegetables may be placed in the pastry case before the filling, separately or in combination:

Leek rings and a pinch of nutmeg, *sautéed*;
Onions, mushrooms, tomato slices, or courgettes, *sautéed*;
Asparagus, sweet corn or spinach, gently cooked.

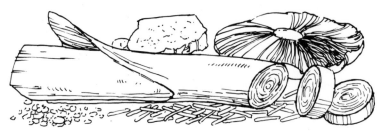

COURGETTE CASSEROLE

Imperial (Metric)
1 lb (½ kilo) courgettes, sliced into thick rings
1 green pepper, sliced
2 large onions, sliced
1 clove garlic, crushed
1 lb (½ kilo) ripe tomatoes, peeled and cut
   into wedges
½ lb (¼ kilo) mushrooms, halved
2-3 sticks celery, chopped
2 tablespoonsful vegetable oil
Pinch of sweet basil
Sea salt and freshly ground black pepper

American
1 lb zucchini, sliced into thick rings
1 green pepper, sliced
2 large onions, sliced
1 clove garlic, crushed
1 lb ripe tomatoes, peeled and cut into
   wedges
4 cupsful mushrooms, halved
2-3 sticks celery, chopped
2½ tablespoonsful vegetable oil
Pinch of sweet basil
Sea salt and freshly ground black pepper

1. *Sauté* the onions and garlic in the oil. Add the rest of the ingredients, cover and cook gently for about 20 minutes.

CURRY SAUCE

Imperial (Metric)
1 onion, sliced
1 green pepper, sliced
¼-½ lb (100g-¼ kilo) mushrooms, sliced
   (optional)
1 clove garlic, crushed with ½ teaspoonful salt
2 tablespoonsful butter
3 teaspoonsful curry powder
1 teaspoonful garam masala
1½ tablespoonsful wholemeal flour
¾ pint (400ml) vegetable stock
2 bay leaves

American
1 onion, sliced
1 green pepper, sliced
2-4 cupsful mushrooms, sliced
   (optional)
1 clove garlic, crushed with ½ teaspoonful salt
2½ tablespoonsful butter
3 teaspoonsful curry powder
1 teaspoonful garam masala
1½ tablespoonsful wholemeal flour
1¾ cupsful vegetable stock
2 bay leaves

1. *Sauté* the onion and green pepper for 5 minutes. Stir in the curry powder and garam masala.

2. Add the mushrooms and cook for 5-10 minutes. Mix in the flour and cook for 1 more minute.

3. Remove the pan from the heat, add the stock, garlic and bay leaves and then bring the sauce to the boil, stirring until smooth and thick. Serve with steamed vegetables, boiled eggs or rice and sambals (page 142).

EGG PIE

Imperial (Metric)	American
1 8 in. pastry case, partly baked	1 8 in. pastry case, partly baked
2 eggs	2 eggs
2-3 tablespoonsful yogurt and/or cream	3 tablespoonsful yogurt and/or cream
Seasoning according to the vegetables used	Seasoning according to the vegetables used

Vegetable Base:
The following vegetables make particularly good fillings for an egg pie:

Sautéed courgettes and onions, leeks, mushrooms, red and green peppers, aubergines; gently cooked spinach, on its own or with onion, sweet corn or asparagus; raw tomato rings.

1. Spread a layer of the vegetables in the pie case, mix the other ingredients and pour them over the vegetables.

2. Garnish with a layer of grated Cheddar or Gruyère cheese, slices of tomato or a sprinkling of seeds. Bake at 300°F/150°C (Gas Mark 2) for 20-30 minutes.

GREEN PEAS AND RICE IN CREAM SAUCE

Imperial (Metric)	American
1 oz (25g) butter	2½ tablespoonsful butter
2 tablespoonsful olive oil	2½ tablespoonsful olive oil
1 large onion or leek, finely diced	1 large onion or leek, finely diced
1 lb (½ kilo) fresh peas, shelled	1 lb fresh peas, shelled
¾ lb (350g) brown rice, well washed	1½ cupsful brown rice, well washed
2 tablespoonsful sesame seeds	2½ tablespoonsful sesame seeds
1½ pints (¾ litre) vegetable stock with a *Huegli* cube	3¾ cupsful vegetable stock with a *Huegli* cube
2 tablespoonsful Parmesan cheese, freshly grated	2½ tablespoonsful Parmesan cheese, freshly grated
¼ pint (150ml) cream	¾ cupful cream
3 spring onions, finely chopped	3 spring onions, finely chopped
Freshly ground black pepper	Freshly ground black pepper

1. Heat the butter and oil in a saucepan and gently cook the onion or leek until transparent.

2. Add the rice and seeds and stir well to coat them with the oil.

3. Add enough stock to cover the rice, then add the peas and cover the saucepan.

4. Lower the heat and leave to simmer for about 20 minutes.

5. Turn off the heat and leave the saucepan covered to gently complete the cooking process. (Add more stock if necessary during cooking, but at the end all the liquid should be absorbed.)

6. Stir in the cream, cheese and pepper and garnish with the spring onions. Serve warm rather than hot or cold.

Variation
Broad beans or French beans may be used instead of peas.

JERUSALEM ARTICHOKES AU GRATIN

Imperial (Metric)	*American*
1 lb (½ kilo) Jerusalem artichokes, well scrubbed	1 lb Jerusalem artichokes, well scrubbed
1 clove	1 clove
Pinch of nutmeg, freshly grated	Pinch of nutmeg, freshly grated
1 onion, finely diced	1 onion, finely diced
2 oz (50g) butter	¼ cupful butter
1 oz (25g) wholemeal flour	¼ cupful wholemeal flour
¼ pint (150ml) milk	¾ cupful milk
1 teaspoonful yeast extract	1 teaspoonful yeast extract
1 oz (25g) fresh wholemeal breadcrumbs	½ cupful fresh wholemeal breadcrumbs

1. Slice the artichokes thickly and cover them with cold water.

2. Add the clove and bring to the boil, then simmer for about 20 minutes. Drain the artichokes and reserve the cooking liquid.

3. Allow the artichokes to cool slightly and then remove the skins. Place the artichokes in an ovenproof dish.

4. Melt half of the butter and stir in the flour. Cook for 1 minute then remove the saucepan from the heat and gradually stir in the milk, whisking continuously.

5. Return the saucepan to the heat and gradually stir in ¼ pint (150ml) of the cooking liquid.

6. Season to taste with sea salt, freshly ground black pepper, the nutmeg and yeast extract.

7. Pour the sauce over the artichokes, top with the breadcrumbs and dot with the remaining butter.

8. Brown lightly in a moderate oven at 350°F/180°C (Gas Mark 4). Serve with a green salad and Lentil Roast.

Variation
Add ½ lb (¼ kilo) of steamed broad beans to the dish, layering them with the artichokes.

LENTIL CROQUETTES

Imperial (Metric)
4 oz (100g) red lentils, cooked
1 onion, diced
2 tablespoonsful parsley, chopped
2 Shredded Wheat sections, crumbled
1 small apple, grated
½ teaspoonful yeast extract
1 egg, beaten
Wholemeal breadcrumbs and sesame seeds
Dried thyme and freshly ground black pepper
   to taste

American
¾ cupful red lentils, cooked
1 onion, diced
2½ tablespoonsful parsley, chopped
2 Shredded Wheat sections, crumbled
1 small apple, grated
½ teaspoonful yeast extract
1 egg, beaten
Wholemeal breadcrumbs and sesame seeds
Dried thyme and freshly ground black pepper
   to taste

1. *Sauté* the onion and combine it with the well mashed lentils.

2. Add the remaining ingredients except for the breadcrumbs and seeds.

3. Shape the mixture into balls and roll them in the breadcrumbs and seeds.

4. Flatten the croquettes gently and fry them at a moderate heat in shallow vegetable until both sides are golden brown.

MARROW WITH PARSLEY STUFFING

Stuffing:

Imperial (Metric)
4 oz (100g) wholemeal breadcrumbs, soaked briefly in warm water
4 oz (100g) nuts, ground or chopped
6 tablespoonsful vegetable oil
2 tablespoonsful parsley, chopped
½ tablespoonful mixed herbs
1 egg, beaten
1 small onion, grated

American
2½ cupsful wholemeal breadcrumbs, soaked briefly in warm water
1 cupful nuts, ground or chopped
7½ tablespoonsful vegetable oil
2½ tablespoonsful parsley, chopped
½ tablespoonful mixed herbs
1 egg, beaten
1 small onion, grated

1. Cut the end off the marrow, scoop out the seeds and parboil it for 5 minutes.

2. Combine all the ingredients for the stuffing and fill the marrow with the mixture. Fix the 'lid' with skewers and brown paper.

3. Bake at 400°F/200°C (Gas Mark 6) for 1 hour. Serve with roast vegetables and tomato gravy.

Tomato Gravy:

Imperial (Metric)	American
½ pint (¼ litre) tomato *purée*	1¼ cupsful tomato *purée*
¼ pint (150ml) water	¾ cupful water
2 tablespoonsful dry sherry	2½ tablespoonsful dry sherry
1 clove garlic, finely crushed	1 clove garlic, finely crushed
1 bay leaf	1 bay leaf
Sea salt and freshly ground black pepper	Sea salt and freshly ground black pepper

1.   Combine the ingredients and simmer for 20 minutes. Remove the bay leaf before serving.

QUICK CASSEROLE

Imperial (Metric)	American
½ lb (¼ kilo) green beans, sliced and cooked, reserving a little cooking water	½ lb green beans, sliced and cooked, reserving a little cooking water
½ lb (¼ kilo) mushrooms, sliced	4 cupsful mushrooms, sliced
1 lb (½ kilo) tomatoes, sliced	1 lb tomatoes, sliced
2 onions, sliced	2 onions, sliced
1 clove garlic, crushed	1 clove garlic, crushed
1 green pepper, sliced	1 green pepper, sliced
1 stick celery, diced	1 stick celery, diced
2 tablespoonsful wheat germ	2½ tablespoonsful wheat germ
Pinch of basil or marjoram	Pinch of basil or marjoram
1 teaspoonful *Marmite* or *Vecon*	1 teaspoonful *Marmite* or *Vecon*
Sea salt and freshly ground black pepper	Sea salt and freshly ground black pepper

1.   *Sauté* the garlic and onions and gradually add the other vegetables.

2.   Stir gently and add the seasoning and *Vecon* or *Marmite* with ¼ pint (150ml) bean stock.

3.   Cover the pan and simmer for 10 minutes, then add the wheat germ and cook for a few more minutes. (The wheat germ thickens the vegetable stock and enriches the savoury flavour of the dish.)

RATATOUILLE

Imperial (Metric)	American
2 tablespoonsful vegetable oil	2½ tablespoonsful vegetable oil
2-3 onions, sliced	2-3 onions, sliced
1-2 cloves garlic, crushed	1-2 cloves, garlic, crushed
1-1½ lb (½-¾ kilo) tomatoes, peeled and sliced	1-1½ lb tomatoes, peeled and sliced
2-4 courgettes, sliced	2-4 zucchini, sliced
2 red or green peppers, sliced	2 red or green peppers, sliced
2 aubergines, unpeeled, diced	2 eggplants, unpeeled, diced
Pinch of raw cane sugar	Pinch of raw cane sugar
Sea salt and freshly ground black pepper	Sea salt and freshly ground black pepper

1. Place the aubergines in a colander and sprinkle with sea salt.

2. Set aside for 30 minutes with a plate and weight on top to squeeze out the bitter juices.

3. Heat the oil over a low heat, add all the ingredients and simmer gently, stirring occasionally until all the vegetables are tender.

4. Serve sprinkled with parsley, or add a few *fresh* green peas. (Marrow may be used to replace the courgettes and the aubergine may be omitted if preferred. This dish is very tasty with crusty wholemeal bread and butter, and may be enjoyed hot or cold.)

SAVOURY PUMPKIN FRITTERS

Imperial (Metric)	American
1 small pumpkin	1 small pumpkin
4 oz (100g) self-raising wholemeal flour	1 cupful self-raising wholemeal flour
2 eggs, beaten	2 eggs, beaten
2 tablespoonsful vegetable oil and a little extra for frying	2½ tablespoonsful vegetable oil and a little extra for frying
1 tablespoonful parsley or mint, chopped	1 tablespoonful parsley or mint, chopped

1. Cut the pumpkin into large wedges and remove the skin.

2. Steam the flesh until tender then pass it through a sieve or chop it up finely.

3. Sift the flour and make a well in the centre.

4. Add the beaten eggs and oil, mix well and fold in ½ lb (¼ kilo) of the pumpkin flesh and the herbs.

5. Season the dough to taste, shape it into balls and flatten the tops.

6. Roll the balls in a little wheat germ, sesame seeds or desiccated coconut if desired.

7. Fry in hot oil until golden brown. Turn the fritters with a spatula and cook the other side.

Note: Sprinkle the fritters with fresh parsley or mint and serve them with a green salad. (Later in the year, parsnips may be used instead of pumpkin.)

STUFFED AUBERGINES

Take ½ large aubergine (eggplant) for each person. Leave the aubergines whole and bake them in a moderate oven at 350°F/180°C (Gas Mark 4) for 20 minutes. Set them aside to cool a little, then cut the aubergines in half lengthways and scoop out the middle two-thirds of the flesh, keeping this for the stuffing.

Imperial (Metric)	American
1 tablespoonful vegetable oil	1 tablespoonful vegetable oil
1 clove garlic, crushed	1 clove garlic, crushed
2 oz (50g) soft, fine wholemeal breadcrumbs	1¼ cupsful soft, fine wholemeal breadcrumbs
4-6 oz (100-200g) tvp, hydrated and drained	½-¾ cupful tvp, hydrated and drained
1 dessertspoonful tomato paste	1 tablespoonful tomato paste
1 egg, beaten	1 egg, beaten
Herbs to taste	Herbs to taste
Freshly ground black pepper	Freshly ground black pepper

1. *Sauté* the onion and garlic in the oil, then add the tvp and the remaining ingredients, except for the egg. Fry for about 10 minutes.

2. Add the aubergine flesh, bind the mixture with the egg, and fill the aubergine shells.

3. Garnish with onion rings and tomato slices and bake for 30-40 minutes at 350°F/180°C (Gas Mark 4). Serve with a salad and fresh wholemeal bread rolls and butter.

Variation
An alternative stuffing may be made by substituting ½ lb (¼ kilo) roughly chopped nuts—brazil, almond, hazel or walnut—and ½ lb (¼ kilo) chopped tomatoes for the tvp and tomato paste.

STUFFED MARROW

Imperial (Metric)	American
1 small marrow (about 6-9 in.)	1 small summer squash (about 6-9 in.)
Cheese Loaf mixture (page 177)	Cheese Loaf mixture (page 177)

1. Halve the marrow. Clean it and cook it gently for about 5 minutes. Drain each half and sprinkle the insides with Parmesan cheese.

2. Stuff the marrow halves with the cheese mixture, sprinkle the tops with Parmesan and bake for 30 minutes at 350°F/180°C (Gas Mark 4). Serve with an onion sauce made from a white sauce (page 136), adding a finely diced onion (*sautéed*) before stirring in the flour.

STUFFED PEPPERS WITH EGGS

Imperial (Metric)
4 large peppers
½ lb (¼ kilo) mushrooms, sliced or chopped
1 large onion, finely diced
1 clove garlic, crushed
1 tablespoonful vegetable oil
4 small eggs
Rosemary and freshly ground black pepper
Grated Cheddar cheese to garnish

American
4 large peppers
4 cupsful mushrooms, sliced or chopped
1 large onion, finely diced
1 clove garlic, crushed
1 tablespoonful vegetable oil
4 small eggs
Rosemary and freshly ground black pepper
Grated Cheddar cheese to garnish

1. Wash and core the peppers and parboil them for about 5 minutes. Drain them thoroughly.

2. Meanwhile, *sauté* the remaining vegetables in the oil, and season.

3. Divide the mixture into the pepper cases and break an egg into each one. Season again with pepper and rosemary and top with the cheese to cover the eggs well.

4. Bake for 15 minutes at 375°F/190°C (Gas Mark 5).

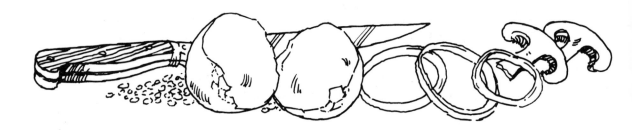

STUFFED PEPPERS WITH RICE

Imperial (Metric)
4 peppers, cored and par-boiled for 5 minutes
3-4 oz (75-100g) brown rice, cooked
1 large onion, diced and *sautéed*
2-3 tomatoes, finely diced and 1 tomato
  sliced into four
Oregano and nutmeg to taste
Grated Parmesan cheese to garnish

American
4 peppers, cored and par-boiled for 5 minutes
1½-2 cupsful brown rice, cooked
1 large onion, diced and *sautéed*
2-3 tomatoes, finely diced and 1 tomato
  sliced into four
Oregano and nutmeg to taste
Grated Parmesan cheese to garnish

1. Sprinkle a little Parmesan cheese into each pepper and shake it to line the inside wall.

2. Combine the remaining ingredients and pile the mixture into the cases.

3. Top each pepper with a thick tomato slice and sprinkle again with Parmesan.

4. Bake for 10-15 minutes to heat through at 350°F/180°C (Gas Mark 4).

TOMATO AND ONION PIE

Imperial (Metric)
4 oz (100g) fresh wholemeal breadcrumbs
4 firm tomatoes, thickly sliced
1 large onion, thinly sliced in rings
Sea salt and freshly ground black pepper
Mixed herbs, dry mustard and a few nuts
   of butter

American
2½ cupsful fresh wholemeal breadcrumbs
4 firm tomatoes, thickly sliced
1 large onion, thinly sliced in rings
Sea salt and freshly ground black pepper
Mixed herbs, dry mustard and a few nuts
   of butter

1. Arrange the ingredients, in the order given, in repeated layers in a buttered ovenproof dish.

2. Bake in a moderate oven at 350°F/180°C (Gas Mark 4) for 30 minutes. Serve in individual dishes as a starter, or as an accompaniment to bland, dry dishes, cauliflower or macaroni cheese.

TOMATOES AND CARROTS

Imperial (Metric)
½ lb (¼ kilo) carrots, diced, ringed or in sticks
1 lb (½ kilo) tomatoes, peeled and chopped
1 large onion, cut into rings
1 bay leaf
Pinch of thyme
Sea salt and freshly ground black pepper

American
1¾ cupsful carrots, diced, ringed or in sticks
1 lb tomatoes, peeled and chopped
1 large onion, cut into rings
1 bay leaf
Pinch of thyme
Sea salt and freshly ground black pepper

1. *Sauté* the onions and carrots. Add the remaining ingredients and a little water. Cover the pan and cook for 20 minutes.

2. Add 1 teaspoonful of *Marmite* or tomato paste and a pinch of raw cane sugar if desired. Serve with buttered egg noodles and chopped parsley.

VEGETABLE SOUFFLÉ

Imperial (Metric)
Approx. ¼ large cauliflower, cut into florets
1-2 carrots, cut into sticks
2-3 oz (50-75g) fresh peas
4 oz (100g) mushrooms, sliced
4 oz (100g) butter +1 dessertspoonful
3 oz (75g) wholemeal flour
1 pint (½ litre) milk
3 eggs, separated
1 tablespoonful wholemeal breadcrumbs
Pinch of freshly grated nutmeg
Sea salt and freshly ground black pepper

American
Approx. ¼ large cauliflower, cut into florets
1-2 carrots, cut into sticks
1 cupful fresh peas
2 cupsful mushrooms, sliced
½ cupful butter +1 dessertspoonful
¾ cupful wholemeal flour
2½ cupsful milk
3 eggs, separated
1 tablespoonful wholemeal breadcrumbs
Pinch of freshly grated nutmeg
Sea salt and freshly ground black pepper

1. Cook the cauliflower, carrots and peas together until just tender.

2. *Sauté* the mushrooms in a little butter for 2 minutes.

3. Melt the rest of the butter, add the flour and cook for 1 minute. Remove the pan from the heat and add the milk gradually, stirring constantly with a wooden spoon until cooked.

4. Season the sauce well, allow it to cool a little and then add the egg yolks, one by one, blending them in well.

5. Stiffly beat the egg whites. Mix the sauce and vegetables together gently, then fold in the egg whites very carefully with a metal spoon.

6. Pour the mixture into a buttered ovenproof dish, sprinkle with the breadcrumbs and bake for 50-60 minutes at 350°F/180°C (Gas Mark 4).

WHEAT AND TOMATO LOAF

Imperial (Metric)
½ lb (¼ kilo) raw wheat, soaked for up to
   12 hours
1½ tablespoonsful vegetable oil
2 large onions, diced
2 eggs, lightly beaten
1 dessertspoonful sage
2-3 sticks celery, chopped
1 green pepper, chopped
2 large tomatoes, chopped

American
1½ cupsful raw wheat, soaked for up to
   12 hours
1½ tablespoonsful vegetable oil
2 large onions, diced
2 eggs, lightly beaten
1 tablespoonful sage
2-3 sticks celery, chopped
1 green pepper, chopped
2 large tomatoes, chopped

1. Cook the wheat by simmering it in salted water for about half an hour.

2. *Sauté* the onions in the oil. Combine all the ingredients and place the mixture in a well oiled ovenproof dish or loaf tin.

3. Bake at 350°F/180°C (Gas Mark 4) for 1 hour. As a variation, nuts may be added to this recipe—about 2 oz (50g) chopped cashews are good. Serve with mushroom sauce (see page 136 for basic recipe).

Sweet Dishes

APPLE CAKE

Imperial (Metric)
4 oz (100g) butter
4 oz (100g) raw cane sugar
2 eggs, beaten
½ lb (¼ kilo) wholemeal flour, sifted
1½ teaspoonful baking powder
Pinch of sea salt
3 apples, peeled and grated
2 tablespoonful raw cane sugar
Grated rind of 1 lemon

American
½ cupful butter
½ cupful raw cane sugar
2 eggs, beaten
2 cupsful wholemeal flour, sifted
1½ teaspoonful baking powder
Pinch of sea salt
3 apples, peeled and grated
2½ tablespoonful raw cane sugar
Grated rind of 1 lemon

1. Cream the butter and 4 oz (100g) of sugar. Add the eggs.

2. Stir in the flour, salt and baking powder and spread half of the mixture in a lined tin.

3. Mix together the apples, sugar and lemon rind, spread this over the cake mixture and then cover with the remaining cake mixture.

4. Bake for 20-30 minutes at 350°F/180°C (Gas Mark 4). While the cake is still warm, brush the top with a mixture of the following ingredients if liked: 1 teaspoonful of cinnamon, 1 tablespoonful of raw cane sugar, the juice of half a lemon.

APPLE SNOW

Imperial (Metric)
3 large green cooking apples, peeled and sliced
1-2 tablespoonsful honey
1 lemon
2-3 egg whites, stiffly beaten

American
3 large green cooking apples, peeled and sliced
1-2 tablespoonsful honey
1 lemon
2-3 egg whites, stiffly beaten

1. Simmer the apples with a piece of lemon peel until cooked. Remove the peel and chill the apples until cold.

2. Add the lemon juice and honey and mix well, adjusting the sweetness if necessary.

3. Fold in the egg whites with a metal spoon. Serve chilled in individual glasses, garnished with a small slice of apple, dipped in lemon juice.

BREAD AND BUTTER PLUMS

Select soft, ripe, juicy plums and halve and stone them. Arrange thick fingers of buttered wholemeal bread in a buttered ovenproof dish and place the fruit on top. Sprinkle with raw cane sugar and dot with butter. Bake for 30 minutes at 350°F/180°C (Gas Mark 4).

CARROT CAKE

Imperial (Metric)
5 eggs, separated
7 oz (200g) honey or Barbados sugar
½ lb (¼ kilo) carrots, grated
½ lb (¼ kilo) almonds, ground
Pinch of cinnamon and powdered clove
2-3 oz (25-50g) wholemeal flour
Grated rind of 1 lemon

American
5 eggs, separated
1 cupful honey or dark brown sugar
1½ cupsful carrots, grated
1½ cupsful almonds, ground
Pinch of cinnamon and powdered clove
⅔ cupful wholemeal flour
Grated rind of 1 lemon

1. Beat the egg yolks and honey until smooth and creamy.

2. Add the remaining ingredients, adding the stiffly beaten egg whites last.

3. Bake in a greased tin for 1 hour at 350°F/180°C (Gas Mark 4).

COTTAGE CHEESE AND PEACHES

For each person use:

Imperial (Metric)
1 fresh peach
1 tablespoonful cottage cheese, sieved
1 tablespoonful ground almonds
¼ teaspoonful clear honey
1 egg, separated

American
1 fresh peach
1 tablespoonful cottage cheese, sieved
1 tablespoonful ground almonds
¼ teaspoonful clear honey
1 egg, separated

1. Arrange the peach halves in a shallow, buttered ovenproof dish.

2. Combine the remaining ingredients, adding the stiffly beaten egg whites last of all.

3. Pile the topping mixture into the peach halves and sprinkle a little cinnamon, garam masala or a few almonds over the top.

4. Bake for 10-20 minutes at 375°F/190°C (Gas Mark 5) until the topping is golden.

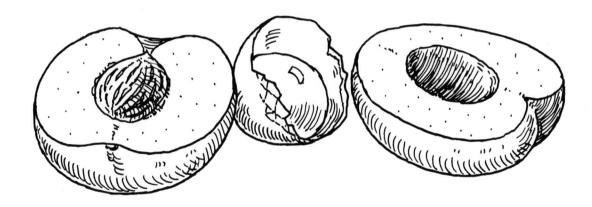

COTTAGE CHEESE WITH PINEAPPLE AND MINT

Imperial (Metric)
½ lb (¼ kilo) cottage cheese, sieved
½ lb (¼ kilo) fresh pineapple, chopped or
  crushed or
1 medium-sized tin pineapples in natural juice
1 dessertspoonful Kirsch
1 tablespoonful fresh mint, chopped
A few sprigs of mint to garnish

American
1 cupful cottage cheese, sieved
1½ cupsful fresh pineapple, chopped or
  crushed or
1 medium-sized tin pineapples in natural juice
1 tablespoonful Kirsch
1 tablespoonful fresh mint, chopped
A few sprigs of mint to garnish

1. Mix the ingredients together well and garnish with the sprigs of fresh mint.

EXOTIC FRUIT SALAD

Imperial (Metric)
½ lb (¼ kilo) lychees, peeled, halved and
   stoned
½ large melon, flesh cut into dice or balls
1-2 Chinese gooseberries, sliced
½ medium-sized pineapple, diced
2 oranges, sliced
1-2 apples, chopped
1 banana, sliced
4 oz (100g) dried apricots and peaches, soaked
Juice of ½-1 lemon

American
2 cupsful lychees, peeled, halved and
   stoned
½ large melon, flesh cut into dice or balls
1-2 Chinese gooseberries, sliced
½ medium-sized pineapple, diced
2 oranges, sliced
1-2 apples, chopped
1 banana, sliced
¾ cupful dried apricots and peaches, soaked
Juice of ½-1 lemon

1. Chop up the soaked apricots and peaches and combine them with the remaining ingredients. (If the dried fruit is particularly good, it may be left in halves.)

FRESH FRUIT SALADS

Basic Ingredients—Any Season
Oranges, red and green apples, bananas, grapes, grapefruit, lemon juice, pears.

Seasonal Additions
Apricots, peaches, cherries, berries, passion fruit, pineapple, mangos, Chinese gooseberries, guavas, plums, nectarines, cantaloupe, honeydew or water melons.

Sweet and Spicy Flavourings
Freshly grated root ginger, nutmeg and cinnamon; honey melted with a little lemon juice; reconstituted dried fruit.

Crunchy Textures
Occasionally add sweet nuts—hazel, almonds or cashews—or a sprinkling of sesame or sunflower seeds.

Garnishes
Experiment with seeds, fresh citrus peel, slices of unpeeled apple in lemon juice; dried fruit, fresh mint and nuts; yogurt, sieved cottage cheese, cream cheese; double, single or soured cream.

Preparation
Use sweetening only occasionally. The fruit should be sweet enough if it is in proper condition.

Prepare the salad as near to the time of eating as possible, at the table if the occasion permits.

Only peel fruit when absolutely necessary.

Use the juice of citrus fruit to prevent apples, pears and bananas going brown.

Peel citrus fruit, preferably with the fingers. Leave on as much pith as you can bear to eat as this contains the bioflavonoids which allow vitamin C to act most efficiently. Cut the fruit between the lines of segments for a pretty, juicy effect, but this may reduce its food value if the salad is not served immediately.

Add berries just before serving as otherwise their bright juice may dye the other ingredients.

Chill the salad, but remove it from the refrigerator ten minutes before serving to allow the flavours to develop fully.

As with savoury salads, give thought to the peculiar properties of each fruit so that you combine them harmoniously.

Beware of fruit, fresh or dried, which has been treated; e.g. waxed citrus and apple peel, sulphur-dried apricots, paraffin-dried currants, sultanas or raisins. Sun-ripened or sun-dried fruit only should be used.

FRUIT CAKE

Imperial (Metric)	American
½ lb (¼ kilo) wholemeal flour	2 cupsful wholemeal flour
3 teaspoonsful baking powder	3 teaspoonsful baking powder
4 oz (100g) Barbados sugar	½ cupful dark brown sugar
¾ lb (350g) currants, raisins and sultanas, mixed	2¼ cupsful currants, raisins and sultanas, mixed
1 oz (25g) mixed peel	¼ cupful mixed peel
1 teaspoonful mixed spice	1 teaspoonful mixed spice
2 large eggs, lightly beaten	2 large eggs, lightly beaten
4 oz (100g) butter, melted	½ cupful butter, melted
¼ pint (150ml) milk	¾ cupful milk
Pinch of each of sea salt and nutmeg	Pinch of each of sea salt and nutmeg

1.   Mix together the flour, baking powder and fruit. Stir in the beaten eggs and melted butter, and add the milk and spices.

2.   Beat well with a wooden spoon until thoroughly mixed. Bake for 2 hours at 300°F/150°C (Gas Mark 2). (Nuts or seeds may be sprinkled over the uncooked mixture.)

FRUIT MOUSSES

A fruit mousse is a blend of fruit *purée*, whipped cream and beaten egg whites, chilled gently. Almost any fruit, dried or fresh, lends itself to mousse making, but the following are particularly delicious: strawberries, raspberries, blackberries, blackcurrants; reconstituted and poached dried apricots, plums, peaches; apples, oranges or lemons.

Apple *purée* may be added to give substance to some berry *purées*, or the juice may be separated from the berries and treated like orange or lemon juice. (Mix 2 teaspoonsful of a vegetarian jelling agent, for example agar-agar, with the juice. Allow it to just begin to set before adding the rest of the ingredients.) Make a thick *purée* of fruit sweetened to taste, approximately ¾ pint (400ml). Using a metal spoon, fold in ½ pint (¼ litre) whipped double cream and 2 large egg whites, stiffly beaten. (Be deft in the blending.) Serve chilled in individual glasses.

FRUIT SALAD COMBINATIONS

Peaches and raspberries.

Cherries, strawberries and raspberries.

Nectarines and strawberries.

Plums and apricots.

Peaches and apricots.

Strawberries or peaches sprinkled with brandy ot white wine;
Cherries sprinkled with Kirsch;
Raspberries sprinkled with *rosé* wine;
Greengages and *vino verde*.

Blueberries and mulberries are best served alone or with cream—especially effective served in tall chilled glasses topped with double cream.

HOME-MADE JAMS

I make very little jam, believing that a diet low in concentrated sugar is best and that most of the value of the fruit is lost in the process of jam making. Just occasionally I make a pot or two when the fruit is abundant, especially for festive breakfasts.

Basic Method

1. Use small quantities of just ripe fruit—firm, and not at all soggy.

2. Clean and chop the fruit and simmer it slowly with water and lemon juice, if used, for about 15-20 minutes before adding the sugar. Bring to the boil, stirring constantly, then boil rapidly, uncovered, to setting point (about 15-20 minutes). (Variations are explained in the following chart.)

3. To test for setting, drop a little of the jam onto a cold saucer. If the sample forms a skin and begins to set as it cools, the jam is ready.

4. Prepare some screw-top jars by scouring and warming; (pour hot water into them or place them in a low oven with the door open). Pour the hot jam into the hot jars.

5. Put a circle of waxed paper directly over the jam in each jar. Seal with screw tops or special cellophane tops.

Fruit	Raw Cane Sugar	Water	Method	Additions
Blackcurrant	1½ × weight of fruit	1 pint (½ litre)/ 2 lb (1 kilo) fruit	Basic	
Damson	1½ × weight of fruit	1 pint (½ litre)/ 1 lb (½ kilo) fruit	Basic; remove stones after simmering fruit	
Apricot	Equal weights	1 tablespoonful/ 1 lb (½ kilo) fruit + juice of 1 lemon/ 2 lb (1 kilo) fruit	Basic	Crack some of the stones and add the kernels.
Gooseberry	1⅓ × weight of fruit	1 pint (½ litre)/ 3 lb (1½ kilo) fruit	Basic	
Rhubarb	Equal weights	None	Basic	Add 2 teaspoonsful ground ginger or 2 tablespoonsful chopped root ginger per lb (½ kilo) fruit.
Raspberry	Equal weights	None	On a flat dish, cover the fruit with the sugar and leave for 1 day. Slowly bring to the boil then boil fast for 3-5 minutes, stirring constantly.	
Strawberry	Equal weights	None Juice of 1 lemon/ 2 lb (1 kilo) fruit	Place the fruit, sugar and juice together in a sauce-pan. Boil for about 15 minutes.	

ICE CREAM

Imperial (Metric)	American
½ pint (¼ litre) double or whipping cream	1¼ cupsful double or whipping cream
Approx. 1 tablespoonful honey	Approx. 1 tablespoonful honey
Few drops of pure vanilla essence or brandy	Few drops of pure vanilla essence or brandy

1. Beat the cream until just holding shape, then add the remaining ingredients.

2. Beat the mixture until stiff and freeze until hard.

PROF. SHEARS' MUESLI

For this recipe, use organically grown cereals, and avoid rye if your body chemistry tends to be acid. Never use a commercial base with skimmed milk and sugar; mix your own from any selection of grains. Combine any or all of the following ingredients, learning to mix the proportions palatably, but try to emphasize those foods which supply individual mineral deficiencies. (In the list below, foods marked with an asterisk should be good for almost everyone. In addition, the combined ingredients provide proteins, unsaturated fats and carbohydrates.)

Sunflower seeds	Magnesium.
Coconut	Silicon, magnesium, calcium, fibre
*Honey/molasses	Iron, copper, silicon, calcium, magnesium, potassium.
Buckwheat	Magnesium.
Millet, sesame, linseed	Potassium.
Barley, crushed oats, caraway seeds	Silicon.
Almonds	Magnesium, manganese.
Walnuts, peanuts	Potassium.
Pecans	Zinc.
Yogurt (unpasteurized)	Calcium, phosphorus, iron and lactic acid (the food of bacteria which transmute other elements into calcium).
*Raisins, sultanas, figs, dried apricots	Iron, copper, calcium, magnesium, silicon.
Pumpkin seeds	Iron, a little magnesium and zinc, hormones useful in prostate troubles and pregnancy.

*Seasonal fruits—two-thirds of the dish	Unconcentrated and alkaline, whereas most other ingredients are acid-forming and concentrated.
*Wheat germ	Copper, B-complex vitamins, vitamin E, fibre.
*Bran	Fibre, zinc.
*Brewers' yeast	B-complex vitamins, vitamin D.
*Kelp	Balanced complement of essential minerals.

PUFFED DELOONS

Imperial (Metric)
½ lb (¼ kilo) wholemeal flour
4 level teaspoonsful baking powder
2 oz (50g) butter
¼ pint (150ml) milk
4 tablespoonsful golden syrup

American
2 cupsful wholemeal flour
4 level teaspoonful baking powder
¼ cupful butter
¾ cupful milk
4 tablespoonsful golden syrup

1. Sift the dry ingredients into a bowl and rub in the butter so that the mixture resembles breadcrumbs.

2. Make a well in the centre and add the milk, mixing to make a soft dough.

3. Turn the dough onto a floured board and knead it lightly before rolling it out to ¾ in. thickness and cutting out small round scones.

4. Melt the golden syrup in a small heavy frying pan and heat it until bubbling but not burning.

5. Drop the scones into the syrup, a few at a time, and cook evenly. Turn the scones over gently as they begin to puff up. The outsides should be very crisp and golden. Serve the scones immediately with butter and lemon juice.

SWEET TOASTED OAT SNACK

Imperial (Metric)	American
6 tablespoonsful rolled oats	7½ tablespoonsful rolled oats
2 tablespoonsful vegetable oil	2½ tablespoonsful vegetable oil
1 tablespoonful honey	1 tablespoonful honey
2 tablespoonsful roughly chopped nuts	2½ tablespoonsful roughly chopped nuts
2 tablespoonsful grated coconut	2½ tablespoonsful grated coconut
3 tablespoonsful dried fruit	4 tablespoonsful dried fruit
2 tablespoonsful sunflower seeds	2 tablespoonsful sunflower seeds

1. Set the oven at 300°F/150°C (Gas Mark 2).

2. Stir the honey and oil together over a low heat. Add the oats and mix well.

3. Spread the mixture loosely over a baking tray and bake for 30 minutes.

4. Set aside to cool and mix in the remaining ingredients. Store in an air-tight jar.

YOGURT

Imperial (Metric)	American
2 tablespoonsful fresh, *live* yogurt	2½ tablespoonsful fresh, *live* yogurt
1 pint (½ litre) milk—raw, skimmed milk preferably	2½ cupsful milk—raw, skimmed milk preferably

1. Heat the milk to blood heat and add the yogurt. (Bacteria multiply best at this temperature so ensure that the container you use to store the mixture in is sterile.)

2. Leave the container in a warm place for 6-8 hours. Try to keep the temperature as constant as possible.

3. When the mixture has thickened a little and tastes right, it is made! Store, well covered, in the refrigerator or some other cold place.

Suitable Yogging Arrangements

A well warmed thermos flask;

A jug covered by a clean tea-towel, left on the kitchen boiler or in the airing cupboard;

A container left over a nite-lite in a cold oven.

For a delicious breakfast dish, mix together the following ingredients:

2 tablespoonsful yogurt;
1 tablespoonful bran;
1 tablespoonful wheat germ;
1 teaspoonful honey;
Fresh fruit.

AUTUMN

Menu Suggestions

1.
Breakfast
Yogurt (p. 112) with stewed apple and wheatgerm

Lunch
Gingered Bean Sprouts and Mushrooms (p. 124)
Dried fruit

Dinner
Autumn Minestrone (p. 121)
Cheese and Olive Flan (p. 135) with Brussels sprouts and tomatoes

2.
Breakfast
Fruit juice and boiled eggs with wholemeal toast, honey and yeast extract

Lunch
Salad of Chinese leaves, Savoy cabbage, peppers, tomatoes and celery
Cheese or left-over flan

Dinner
Brazil Nut and Tomato Loaf (p. 134)
or
Chick Pea and Mushroom Pie (p. 136) with steamed carrots, parsnips and cabbage
Tropical Fruit Salad (p. 154)

3.
Breakfast
Apple or peach
Wholemeal toast and peanut butter
or
Sunflower spread
or
Tahini and honey

Lunch
Carrot and Apple Salad (p. 127) with cottage cheese
Banana and hazelnuts (p. 147)

Dinner
Mixed Vegetables and Tomatoes (p. 139) with Chinese leaves or grated raw cabbage
Baked Stuffed Potatoes (p. 133)
Pineapple Slices (p. 153)

4.
Breakfast
Fruit, yogurt (p. 112), tahini and seeds

Lunch
Mushroom Soup (p. 126)
Cole-slaw (p. 128) with wholemeal bread and butter

Dinner
Lasagne (p. 138) with green salad
Apples, figs and dates

5.
Breakfast
Vegetable juice
Wholemeal toast, butter, tomatoes and black pepper

Lunch
Apple and Pear Fruit Salad (p. 147)
Dried fruit and nuts

Dinner
Pancake Omelette (p. 140) stuffed with *sautéed* peppers, tomatoes or courgettes
Steamed carrots and broccoli
Walnut and Orange Salad (p. 154)

6.
Breakfast
Fresh pears or bananas with cream or yogurt (p. 112)

Lunch
Cream of Onion Soup (p. 123)
Salad of fresh seed sprouts, tomato, watercress and parsley with wholemeal bread

Dinner
Crudités and Cocktail Sauce (p. 124)
Butter Bean Fritters (p. 134)
or
Grain and Bean Risotto (p. 138) with steamed greens and gravy

7.
Breakfast
Grapefruit juice, poached egg on wholemeal toast

Lunch
Cauliflower, mushroom and celery salad in tomato dressing (p. 86)
Lactic cheese

Dinner
Avocado and Mushroom Entrée (p. 122) with thin wholewheat crispbread
Vegetable Sauce II (p. 145) with wholewheat spaghetti and grated cheese

8.
Breakfast
Yogurt (p. 112) and dried apricots (reconstituted)

Lunch
Carrot, celery and apple salad with walnuts and wholemeal bread and butter

Dinner
Cottage Cheese and Oat Loaf (p. 137) with steamed carrots and spinach
Bunch of grapes

9.
Breakfast
Egg Nog (p. 150)
Apple or pear

Lunch
Jacket baked potato
Salad of peppers, lettuce and cucumber in yogurt dressing (p. 32)

Dinner
Paprika 'Beef' (p. 141)
Brussels sprouts, onions and parsnips
Cottage Cheese and Almonds (p. 148)

10.
Breakfast
Compote of grapefruit, oranges and grapes

Lunch
Autumn Glory Soup (p. 122)
Wholewheat crispbread with lactic, cottage or curd cheese and French mustard
Pear

Dinner
Savoury Stuffed Marrow (p. 143)
Baked Onions (p. 132) and steamed vegetables
Port Wine Apples (p. 153) and cream

11.
Breakfast
Half a grapefruit
Yogurt (p. 112)

Lunch
Beetroot Salad (p. 127) in soured cream or French dressing (p. 171)
Wholemeal bread and butter

Dinner
Leek and Potato Soup (p. 125)
Compote of steamed vegetables garnished with watercress,
cashew nuts and grated cheese
Chocolate Mousse (p. 148)

12.
Breakfast
Stewed dried apricots sprinkled with milled nuts and ground almonds

Lunch
Mushroom and Celery Salad (p. 129)
Green salad with a cheese board

Dinner
Sweet Spicy Curry (p. 144) with sambals (p. 142)
Almond and Pepper Rice (p. 131)
or
plain brown rice
Fresh fruit
or
Orange and Lemon Sauce (p. 153) with Ice Cream (p. 110)

13.
Breakfast
Boiled egg with wholemeal toast
Fresh fruit

Lunch
Salad of celery, carrot and seed sprouts with nuts or grated cheese
Wholemeal bread, butter or *Barmene*

Dinner
Marrow and Apple Soup (p. 125)
Saturday Night Special (p. 142)

14.
Breakfast
Fresh citrus *compote*

Lunch
Jacket baked potato with watercress
Tomato and Mushroom Salad (p. 85)

Dinner
Cabbage and Tomatoes (p. 135)
or
Sweet Corn Casserole (p. 143)
Spicy Apple or Banana Pudding (p. 154)

Starters

AUTUMN MINESTRONE

Imperial (Metric)	American
1 onion, sliced	1 onion, sliced
1 clove garlic, crushed	1 clove garlic, crushed
3 sticks celery, chopped	3 sticks celery, chopped
2 carrots, diced	2 carrots, diced
2 leeks, sliced	2 leeks, sliced
½ small cabbage, shredded	½ small cabbage, shredded
½ small marrow, diced	½ summer squash, diced
½ lb (¼ kilo) tomatoes, skinned and chopped	2 cupsful tomatoes, skinned and chopped
4 oz (100g) wholemeal spaghetti	1 cupful (raw) wholemeal spaghetti
3-4 pints (1½-2 litres) vegetable stock	7½-10 cupsful vegetable stock
Pinch each of parsley, rosemary, basil and oregano	Pinch each of parsley, rosemary, basil and oregano
Sea salt and freshly ground black pepper	Sea salt and freshly ground black pepper
Parmesan cheese to garnish	Parmesan cheese to garnish

1. Simmer the onion, garlic, celery and carrot in the stock for 30 minutes.

2. Add the remaining vegetables, herbs and broken spaghetti and simmer for a further 30 minutes.

3. Season to taste and sprinkle Parmesan cheese into the serving bowls.

Variation
A small quantity of calabrese could be included with or instead of the cabbage.

AUTUMN GLORY SOUP

Imperial (Metric)
1 pint (½ litre) tomato juice
1 pint (½ litre) vegetable stock
1 large onion, diced
3 carrots, cut in rings
3 tablespoonful barley, soaked in water
   for 12-24 hours
1 teaspoonful each oregano and sweet basil
½ pint (¼ litre) milk
1 tablespoonful butter
Selection of green vegetables
Dash of freshly ground black pepper

American
2½ cupsful tomato juice
2½ cupsful vegetable stock
1 large onion, diced
3 carrots, cut in rings
4 tablespoonsful barley, soaked in water
   for 12-24 hours
1 teaspoonful each oregano and sweet basil
1¼ cupsful milk
1 tablespoonful butter
Selection of green vegetables
Dash of freshly ground black pepper

1. Combine all the ingredients except for the milk and butter in a large saucepan. Cover and simmer gently for 40 minutes.

2. Add the milk and butter, mix well and serve. (Never allow liquid with milk in it to boil or the milk will curdle.)

AVOCADO AND MUSHROOM ENTRÉE

Imperial (Metric)
2 avocados
2-4 oz (50-100g) mushrooms, finely chopped
2 tablespoonsful oil and vinegar dressing
   (page 30)

American
2 avocados
1-2 cupsful mushrooms, finely chopped
2½ tablespoonsful oil and vinegar dressing
   (page 30)

1. Halve the avocados and remove the stones, then pile the mushrooms into the groove.

2. Sprinkle with the oil and vinegar dressing and top with finely chopped spring onions or chives, if liked.

CELERY AND MUSHROOM ENTRÉE

Imperial (Metric)	American
1 stick celery per person	1 stick celery per person
2 tablespoonful butter or polyunsaturated margarine	2½ tablespoonful butter or polyunsaturated margarine
4 oz (100g) mushrooms	2 cupsful mushrooms
¼ pint (150ml) soured cream	¾ cupful soured cream
2 oz (50g) cheese, grated	¾ cupful cheese, grated
Vegetable stock or white wine	Vegetable stock or white wine
Sea salt and freshly ground black pepper	Sea salt and freshly ground black pepper

1. Cut the celery into 1 in. pieces and layer it with the pepper, salt and enough stock or wine to moisten in an ovenproof dish.

2. Dot the celery with butter, cover and bake in a moderate oven at 350°F/180°C (Gas Mark 4) for 20 minutes.

3. *Sauté* the mushrooms and scatter them over the celery.

4. Pour the soured cream over the dish, then sprinkle with grated cheese and brown under the grill.

CREAM OF ONION SOUP

Imperial (Metric)	American
1 lb (½ kilo) onions, chopped	4 cupsful onions, chopped
2 tablespoonful freshly chopped parsley	2½ tablespoonful freshly chopped parsley
1 teaspoonful dried sage	1 teaspoonful dried sage
1 oz (25g) butter	2½ tablespoonful butter
1 oz (25g) wholemeal flour	¼ cupful wholemeal flour
1 pint (½ litre) milk	2½ cupsful milk
Sea salt and freshly ground black pepper	Sea salt and freshly ground black pepper

1. Simmer the onions with the herbs in ½ pint (¼ litre) of water until tender.

2. Pass the onions through a sieve or liquidize them.

3. Melt the butter, stir in the flour and cook for about 1 minute.

4. Remove the pan from the heat and gradually stir in half of the milk, then the onion *purée*. Gradually add the remaining milk stirring constantly as the soup thickens.

5. Season to taste and serve with *croûtons* of fried wholemeal bread or with grated cheese and chopped parsley.

Note: This recipe may also be used with leeks instead of onions.

CRUDITÉS AND COCKTAIL SAUCE

Imperial (Metric)
4 tablespoonsful mayonnaise (page 172)
2 tablespoonsful each yogurt and thick cream
  or
4 tablespoonsful yogurt
2 teaspoonsful lemon juice
1 teaspoonful *Holbrook's* Worcester sauce
Dash of *Tabasco* sauce
Sea salt and freshly ground black pepper

If used with rice salad add:

2 tablespoonsful vegetable oil
1 tablespoonful cider vinegar

American
5 tablespoonsful mayonnaise (page 172)
2½ tablespoonsful each yogurt and thick cream
  or
5 tablespoonsful yogurt
2½ teaspoonsful lemon juice
1 teaspoonful *Holbrook's* Worcester sauce
Dash of *Tabasco* sauce
Sea salt and freshly ground black pepper

2½ tablespoonsful vegetable oil
1 tablespoonful cider vinegar

1. Blend the ingredients thoroughly and set aside to chill.

2. Serve with chilled, quartered hard-boiled eggs, sliced mushrooms, chilled, cooked green beans, with lettuce, diced cucumber, celery, lemon wedges and buttered wholemeal bread.

GINGERED BEAN SPROUTS AND MUSHROOMS

For each person use:

Imperial (Metric)
4 oz (100g) bean sprouts (mung or aduki are
  excellent)
2 oz (50g) mushrooms, sliced
½ teaspoonful fresh stem ginger, chopped
½ clove garlic, crushed
Soy sauce to taste
A little vegetable oil

American
2 cupsful bean sprouts (mung or aduki are
  excellent)
1 cupful mushrooms, sliced
½ teaspoonful fresh stem ginger, chopped
½ clove garlic, crushed
Soy sauce to taste
A little vegetable oil

1. Heat the oil in a pan and *sauté* the bean sprouts and mushrooms briefly.

2. Add the ginger, garlic and soy sauce to taste and stir-fry for about 5 minutes.

LEEK AND POTATO SOUP

Imperial (Metric)
1 lb (½ kilo) leeks, cleaned, trimmed and cut into rings
1 lb (½ kilo) potatoes, peeled and roughly diced
1-2 oz (50g) butter
1½ pints (¾ litre) cold water
1-2 egg yolks beaten into
4 tablespoonsful cream (optional)
Pinch of nutmeg
Sea salt and freshly ground black pepper
Chopped parsley or mint to garnish

American
1 lb leeks, cleaned, trimmed and cut into rings
1 lb potatoes, peeled and roughly diced
3-5 tablespoonsful butter
3¾ cupsful cold water
1-2 egg yolks beaten into
5 tablespoonsful cream (optional)
Pinch of nutmeg
Sea salt and freshly ground black pepper
Chopped parsley or mint to garnish

1. *Sauté* the leeks in the butter and then add the potatoes. Cook the vegetables for 3-4 minutes but do not allow them to brown.

2. Add the seasoning and the water, then cover the pan and simmer the potatoes for 30-40 minutes or until they are very well cooked.

3. When the soup is cool, liquidize the ingredients or pass them through a sieve and then return them to the saucepan.

4. If the cream and eggs are to be added, blend them with a few spoonsful of the soup before adding them gradually to the saucepan. Do not boil or even overheat the mixture as this will cause it to curdle.

5. Serve garnished with parsley, mint or leek rings, separately *sautéed*.

MARROW AND APPLE SOUP

Imperial (Metric)
1 large marrow, peeled and seeded
1 lb (½ kilo) Bramley apples, quartered and cored
2 onions, diced
1 oz (25g) butter
1½-2 pints (¾-1 litre) vegetable stock
1 clove
¼ pint (150ml) cream

American
1 summer squash, peeled and seeded
1 lb Bramley apples, quartered and cored
2 onions, diced
2½ tablespoonsful butter
3¾-5 cupsful vegetable stock
1 clove
¾ cupful cream

1. Cut the marrow flesh into cubes and simmer in half of the stock for about 15 minutes.

2. *Sauté* the onion in the butter until transparent. Add the apples, clove and remaining stock. Cover the pan and simmer for 30-40 minutes until tender.

3. Sieve or blend the mixture, add it to the marrow and reheat.

4. Add the cream just before serving.

MUSHROOM SOUP

Imperial (Metric)
1 lb (½ kilo) field mushrooms, peeled and
   chopped
½ pint (¼ litre) vegetable stock
1 small onion, sliced
1 oz (25g) butter
1 oz (25g) wholemeal flour
¾ pint (400ml) milk
1 egg yolk, beaten

American
8 cupsful field mushrooms, peeled and
   chopped
1¼ cupsful vegetable stock
1 small onion, sliced
2½ tablespoonsful butter
⅓ cupful wholemeal flour
1¾ cupful milk
1 egg yolk, beaten

1. Simmer the onion and mushrooms in the stock for 30 minutes. Sieve or liquidize them if you prefer a smooth soup.

2. Melt the butter, stir in the flour and cook gently for 1 minute.

3. Remove the pan from the heat to stir in the milk, seasoning and mushroom stock. Simmer for quarter of an hour.

4. Set aside to cool a little, then stir in the beaten egg yolk. Do not boil the soup as this will curdle the egg.

5. Serve garnished with extra *sautéed* mushrooms and/or cream or dry sherry.

Salads and Salad Dressings

BEETROOT SALAD

Imperial (Metric)
1 lb (½ kilo) raw beetroot, peeled and grated
  coarsely
2 oz (50g) fresh parsley, finely chopped
Soured cream or yogurt dressing (page 32)

American
1 lb raw beetroot, peeled and grated
  coarsely
1 cupful fresh parsley, finely chopped
Soured cream or yogurt dressing (page 32)

1. Combine the ingredients and garnish with a few sprigs of parsley.

CARROT AND APPLE SALAD

Imperial (Metric)
3 large carrots, grated coarsely
1 large green apple, sliced finely
4 oz (100g) cottage cheese
2 tablespoonsful oil and vinegar or
  lemon juice dressing (pages 30 and 84)

American
3 large carrots, grated coarsely
1 large green apple, sliced finely
½ cupful cottage cheese
2½ tablespoonsful oil and vinegar or
  lemon juice dressing (pages 30 and 84)

1. Combine the ingredients thoroughly.

COLE-SLAW

Imperial (Metric)
1 medium-sized red or green cabbage, shredded
2 carrots, grated
1 onion, diced finely
3 oz (75g) dried fruit
3 oz (75g) green or black olives, sliced
3 sticks celery, sliced finely into crescents
1 pepper, cut into rings
1 large apple, diced coarsely

American
1 medium-sized red or green cabbage, shredded
2 carrots, grated
1 onion, diced finely
¾ cupful dried fruit
½ cupful green or black olives, sliced
3 sticks celery, sliced finely into crescents
1 pepper, cut into rings
1 large apple, diced coarsely

1. Combine the ingredients well with a mixture of 2-3 tablespoonsful of mayonnaise and 1-2 tablespoonsful of oil and vinegar dressing (pages 172 and 30) or use the cole-slaw dressing (see below).

COLE-SLAW DRESSING

Imperial (Metric)
6 tablespoonsful vegetable oil
1 tablespoonful lemon juice
1 tablespoonful orange juice
1 tablespoonful *Holbrook's* Worcester sauce
2 tablespoonsful onion, finely chopped
1 tablespoonful olives, chopped
1 tablespoonful parsley, chopped
½ teaspoonful dry mustard

American
7½ tablespoonsful vegetable oil
1 tablespoonful lemon juice
1 tablespoonful orange juice
1 tablespoonful *Holbrook's* Worcester sauce
2½ tablespoonsful onion, finely chopped
1 tablespoonful olives, chopped
1 tablespoonful parsley, chopped
½ teaspoonful dry mustard

1. Combine the ingredients thoroughly.

LEMON JUICE DRESSING

Juice of 1 lemon;
Pimento and raw cane sugar to taste;
Sea salt and freshly ground black pepper.

1. Combine the ingredients thoroughly.

MUSHROOM AND CELERY SALAD

Imperial (Metric)
1 lb (½ kilo) fresh button mushrooms, halved
   or quartered
2-3 sticks celery, finely sliced into crescents

American
8 cupsful fresh button mushrooms, halved or
   quartered
2-3 sticks celery, finely sliced into crescents

1. Marinate the ingredients well in either French dressing (page 171) or lemon juice dressing (page 128) with rosemary.

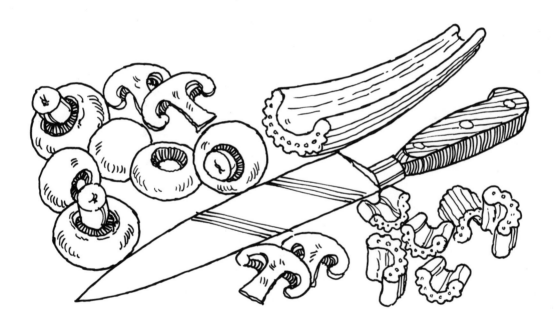

Savoury Dishes

ALMOND AND PEPPER RICE

Imperial (Metric)
¾ lb (350g) short-grained brown rice
2 tablespoonsful vegetable oil
1-2 large onions, diced
1 clove garlic, crushed
½ teaspoonful turmeric
1¼ pints (650ml) vegetable stock made with
   Vecon, *Tastex* or *Marmite*
1 large green pepper, sliced
4 oz (100g) whole almonds, toasted in the oven
3 tablespoonsful fresh parsley, chopped
Freshly ground black pepper

American
1½ cupsful short-grained brown rice
2½ tablespoonsful vegetable oil
1-2 large onions, diced
1 clove garlic, crushed
½ teaspoonful turmeric
3¼ cupsful vegetable stock made with
   Vecon, *Tastex* or *Marmite*
1 large green pepper, sliced
¾ cupful whole almonds, toasted in the oven
4 tablespoonsful fresh parsley, chopped
Freshly ground black pepper

1. Fry the onion, garlic and turmeric in the oil until the onion is soft but not browned.

2. Add the rice and coat it well with the oil, then add the stock. Bring to the boil, then lower the heat and cook, covered, for about 30-40 minutes until all the water is absorbed.

3. Check the seasoning and add the black pepper and parsley, mixing thoroughly.

4. Gently toss the green pepper and almonds through the rice, leaving some to garnish the dish before serving.

Note: This may be served as an accompaniment to a curry dish or vegetable casserole.

ALMOND-STUFFED MARROW

Imperial (Metric)	American
1 medium-sized marrow	1 summer squash
4 oz (100g) ground almonds	1 cupful ground almonds
4 oz (100g) wholemeal breadcrumbs	2½ cupsful wholemeal breadcrumbs
2 eggs, beaten with 2 tablespoonsful water	2 eggs, beaten with 2 tablespoonsful water
2-3 onions, diced	2-3 onions, diced
2 tablespoonsful vegetable oil	2½ tablespoonsful vegetable oil
Pinch of marjoram	Pinch of marjoram
2 tablespoonsful skimmed milk powder	2½ tablespoonsful skimmed milk powder
2 tablespoonsful tomato paste	2½ tablespoonsful tomato paste
2 tomatoes and a few whole almonds to garnish	2 tomatoes and a few whole almonds to garnish
Sea salt and freshly ground black pepper	Sea salt and freshly ground black pepper

1. Halve and de-seed the marrow, boil it for 10 minutes and leave it to drain.

2. *Sauté* the onions in the oil, then mix them with all the ingredients, except the tomato paste, to a wet consistency.

3. Spread the marrow cases with tomato paste and pile in the filling.

4. Garnish with a row of tomato slices, each one topped with an almond, and bake for 30 minutes at 350°F/180°C (Gas Mark 4).

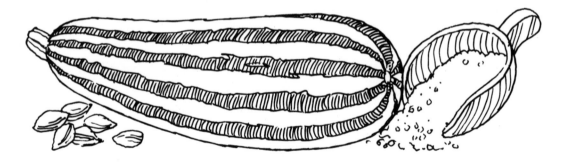

BAKED ONIONS

Imperial (Metric)	American
1 large, firm onion per person	1 large, firm onion per person
A little vegetable oil	A little vegetable oil
Sage	Sage

1. Peel each onion, flattening the base so that it stands upright.

2. Rub the onions with oil and place them in a lightly oiled baking dish.

3. Sprinkle each one liberally with sage and bake at 350°F/180°C (Gas Mark 4) for 50-60 minutes. (These are particularly good served with Topped Tomatoes or Stuffed Marrow, pages 26 and 99.)

BAKED STUFFED POTATOES

1. Scrub the potatoes, one per person, and bake them at 375°F/190°C (Gas Mark 5) until well done (about 1½ hours, depending on size).

2. Remove them from the oven, wrap in a tea-towel for a few minutes, then cut each one in half, scooping the flesh out into a large bowl.

3. Mash the potato thoroughly and gradually beat in the following ingredients in any combination:

A little warmed milk;
A large nut of butter;
Pinch of nutmeg;
Freshly ground black pepper;
Sea salt.

Variations

2-4 tablespoonsful yogurt or cream cheese;
Grated Cheddar, Swiss or cottage cheese;
Grated onion or chopped spring onion;
Chopped parsley;
Sautéed, sliced mushrooms;
A sprinkling of herbs.

To Garnish:

A sprinkling of cayenne pepper or nutmeg;
Grated Cheddar, Swiss or Parmesan cheese;
Fresh wholemeal breadcrumbs with a nut of butter.

Serve with:

Sweet Corn Casserole (page 143);
A green mixed salad

BRAZIL NUT AND TOMATO LOAF

Imperial (Metric)
4 oz (100g) each almonds and Brazil nuts,
    ground or
½ lb (¼ kilo) Brazil nuts, ground
½ lb (¼ kilo) soft wholemeal breadcrumbs
1 egg, beaten
1 tablespoonful tomato paste
1 large onion, diced finely
1 clove garlic, crushed
Sea salt and freshly ground black pepper
Pinch of marjoram

American
1 cupful each almonds and Brazil nuts,
    ground or
2 cupsful Brazil nuts, ground
5 cupsful soft wholemeal breadcrumbs
1 egg, beaten
1 tablespoonful tomato paste
1 large onion, diced finely
1 clove garlic, crushed
Sea salt and freshly ground black pepper
Pinch of marjoram

1. Gently simmer the onion and garlic in a small amount of water. When transparent, combine them with the remaining ingredients.

2. Fill a loaf tin or a shallow dish with the mixture and bake for 40 minutes at 350°F/180°C (Gas Mark 4). Serve with vegetables. (This is also very good served cold with salad or steamed broccoli.)

BUTTER BEAN FRITTERS

Imperial (Metric)
4 oz (100g) butter beans
1 onion, diced
1 carrot, grated
2 oz (50g) hard cheese, grated
1 egg, beaten
1 teaspoonful yeast extract
2 Weetabix (or similar), crushed
Herbs or curry powder to taste
Wholemeal breadcrumbs for coating
Vegetable oil for frying

American
½ cupful navy beans
1 onion, diced
1 carrot, grated
½ cupful hard cheese, grated
1 egg, beaten
1 teaspoonful yeast extract
2 Weetabix (or similar), crushed
Herbs or curry powder to taste
Wholemeal breadcrumbs for coating
Vegetable oil for frying

1. Cook, drain and mash the beans, *sauté* the onions in a little vegetable oil and mix the ingredients, using the egg to bind them.

2. Divide the mixture into sausage shapes and roll them in the breadcrumbs.

3. Fry in shallow vegetable oil.

CABBAGE AND TOMATOES

Imperial (Metric)
2 large onions, diced
2 cloves garlic, crushed
1 small cabbage, sliced
2 sticks celery, sliced
4 large red tomatoes, cut in wedges
2 tablespoonsful vegetable oil
Fines herbes and oregano
Freshly ground black pepper

American
2 large onions, diced
2 cloves garlic, crushed
1 small cabbage, sliced
2 sticks celery, sliced
4 large red tomatoes, cut in wedges
2½ tablespoonsful vegetable oil
Fines herbes and oregano
Freshly ground black pepper

1. In a covered pan, soften the onion and garlic in a little oil. Add the remaining ingredients and cook, covered, over a low heat for about 15 minutes.

2. Cheese may be sprinkled over this for the last few minutes of cooking, or grated cheese and bran mixed together may be added after cooking. If so, the whole dish should be grilled briefly to melt the cheese.

CHEESE AND OLIVE FLAN

Pastry:

Imperial (Metric)
½-¾ lb (225-350g) wholemeal flour
2 tablespoonsful sesame seeds
4-5 tablespoonsful vegetable oil

American
2-3 cupsful wholemeal flour
2½ tablespoonsful sesame seeds
5-6 tablespoonsful vegetable oil

1. Sift the flour and rub in the oil and seeds. Moisten with a little cold water and knead gently. Roll out the pastry and spread it over an oiled shallow dish. Bake for 15 minutes at 400°F/200°C (Gas Mark 6).

Filling:

4-6 eggs
½ lb (¼ kilo) cottage cheese, sieved
3 oz (75g) Cheddar or Swiss cheese, grated
2-3 tablespoonsful olives, chopped
¼ pint (150ml) water
Sea salt and freshly ground black pepper

4-6 eggs
1 cupful cottage cheese, sieved
1 cupful Cheddar or Swiss cheese, grated
3 tablespoonsful olives, chopped
¾ cupful water
Sea salt and freshly ground black pepper

1. Blend all the ingredients together and pour the mixture into the pastry case.

2. Top with sesame seeds or grated cheese and bake for 30 minutes at 300°F/150°C (Gas Mark 2). Serve with whole red tomatoes and a green salad or any selection of vegetables.

CHEESE SAUCE

This recipe may be used to make a white sauce by omitting the cheese.

Imperial (Metric)
6 oz (200g) Cheddar or Swiss cheese, grated
1 oz (25g) wholemeal wheat flour or rice flour
2 tablespoonsful butter or vegetable oil
½-¾ pint (275-400ml) milk or milk and
  vegetable stock
Pinch of cayenne pepper and dry mustard
  or mace
Sea salt and freshly ground black pepper

American
2 cupsful Cheddar or Swiss cheese, grated
¼ cupful wholemeal wheat flour or rice flour
2½ tablespoonsful butter or vegetable oil
1¼-1¾ cupsful milk or milk and vegetable
  stock
Pinch of cayenne pepper and dry mustard
  or mace
Sea salt and freshly ground black pepper

1. Heat the butter or oil gently, then remove from the heat and add the flour.

2. Cook over a low heat for 1 minute, stirring constantly with a wooden spoon.

3. Gradually add the liquid, a little at a time, continuing to stir until the mixture coats the spoon and is smooth and glossy.

4. Gradually stir in the cheese and season well. (For extra richness, add a beaten egg, a little cream or a nut of butter and beat well.)

Note: This sauce may be served with a selection of steamed vegetables or wholemeal macaroni. Top with extra grated cheese and/or seeds and bake in a moderate oven at 350°F/180°C (Gas Mark 4) to brown the top.

CHICK PEA AND MUSHROOM PIE

Imperial (Metric)
½ lb (¼ kilo) chick peas, cooked until tender
½ lb (¼ kilo) mushrooms, sliced
1 onion, diced
1 carrot, sliced
1 tablespoonful vegetable oil
1 oz (25g) wholemeal flour
½ pint (¼ litre) water
1 teaspoonful tomato *purée*
1 teaspoonful *Tastex*
1 vegetable stock cube
1 teaspoonful soy sauce

American
1 cupful garbanzo beans, cooked until tender
4 cupsful mushrooms, sliced
1 onion, diced
1 carrot, sliced
1 tablespoonful vegetable oil
¼ cupful wholemeal flour
1¼ cupsful water
1 teaspoonful tomato *purée*
1 teaspoonful *Tastex*
1 vegetable stock cube
1 teaspoonful soy sauce

1. *Sauté* the onion and carrot in the oil for 20 minutes. Add the mushrooms and cook for a further 5 minutes.

2. Stir in the flour, cook for 1 minute and gradually add the flavourings and water. Cook for 3-4 minutes more.

3. Add the peas and place the mixture in a greased ovenproof dish.

Crumble Topping:

2 tablespoonsful cheese, grated	2½ tablespoonsful cheese, grated
1 tablespoonful ground almonds	1 tablespoonful ground almonds
1 tablespoonful sesame seeds	1 tablespoonful sesame seeds
1 tablespoonful desiccated coconut	1 tablespoonful desiccated coconut

1. Combine the ingredients and spread the topping over the chick pea and mushroom base.

2. Bake in a moderate oven at 350°F/180°C (Gas Mark 4) for 20-30 minutes until the top is golden brown.

COTTAGE CHEESE AND OAT LOAF

Imperial (Metric)
¾ lb (350g) cottage cheese
½ lb (¼ kilo) rolled oats
1½ tablespoonsful bran
1 dessertspoonful *fines herbes*
1 teaspoonful sage
3 large eggs, lightly beaten
½ teaspoonful mustard
2 large onions, diced finely
2 cloves garlic, crushed
1 tablespoonful vegetable oil
Dash of cayenne pepper
Sea salt to taste

American
1½ cupsful cottage cheese
2 cupsful rolled oats
1½ tablespoonsful bran
1 tablespoonful *fines herbes*
1 teaspoonful sage
3 large eggs, lightly beaten
½ teaspoonful mustard
2 large onions, diced finely
2 cloves garlic, crushed
1 tablespoonful vegetable oil
Dash of cayenne pepper
Sea salt to taste

1. *Sauté* the onions and garlic in the oil. Combine all the ingredients, adding a little more oats or bran if necessary.

2. Mix thoroughly and place in a well oiled, ovenproof dish. Cover with sesame seeds or bran and bake for 1 hour at 250°F/130°C (Gas Mark ½). (This dish is very good served warm or cold with salads.)

GRAIN AND BEAN RISOTTO

Imperial (Metric)
4-6 oz (100-200g) soya beans, soaked overnight
4-6 oz (100-200g) whole wheat, soaked
  overnight
10 oz (300g) short-grained rice
1 large onion, diced
1 large clove garlic, crushed
2 large carrots, sliced into sticks
4 sticks celery, chopped coarsley
2 tablespoonsful fennel, chopped (optional)
1 teaspoonful caraway seeds
1 teaspoonful poppy seeds
2 tablespoonsful sunflower oil
2 pints (1 litre) cold water or vegetable stock
Soy sauce and *Tabasco* sauce to taste

American
⅔ cupful soya beans, soaked overnight
⅔ cupful whole wheat, soaked
  overnight
1¼ cupsful short-grained rice
1 large onion, diced
1 large clove garlic, crushed
2 large carrots, sliced into sticks
4 sticks celery, chopped coarsely
2½ tablespoonsful fennel, chopped (optional)
1 teaspoonful caraway seeds
1 teaspoonful poppy seeds
2½ tablespoonsful sunflower oil
5 cupsful cold water or vegetable stock
Soy sauce and *Tabasco* sauce to taste

1. Boil the soya beans for at least 10 minutes, then reduce the heat and cook until tender.

2. Using a large, heavy pan, heat the oil, add the onion and garlic and stir until transparent.

3. Stir in the rice, coating it with the oil, then add the other ingredients, mixing in the water gradually.

4. Cover and cook over a low heat for 40-50 minutes.

LASAGNE

Imperial (Metric)
4 oz (100g) wholemeal lasagne noodles
1 quantity of Vegetable Sauce (page 145)
½ pint (¼ litre) cheese sauce (page 136)
Grated Parmesan cheese
Slices of tomato to garnish

American
4 oz wholemeal lasagne noodles
1 quantity of Vegetable Sauce (page 145)
1¼ cupsful cheese sauce (page 136)
Grated Parmesan cheese
Slices of tomato to garnish

1. Cook the pasta and arrange it with the vegetables and cheese sauce in repeated layers in a buttered ovenproof dish.

2. Top with slices of tomato and sprinkle with Parmesan cheese. Bake until golden in a moderate oven at 350°F/180°C (Gas Mark 4) for 20-30 minutes.

Note: Lasagne noodles need not be cooked separately before assembling the dish if the vegetable sauce has a little more liquid than usual and if there is plenty of time for the dish to stand before baking. I often assemble it in the morning for serving in the evening.

MIXED VEGETABLES
AND TOMATOES

Imperial (Metric)
1 large onion, sliced
1 clove garlic, crushed
2 carrots, cut into sticks
2 potatoes, diced
4 oz (100g) mushrooms, sliced
3 sticks celery, chopped
1 lb (½ kilo) ripe tomatoes, skinned and
    chopped
1 green pepper, sliced in rings
1 teaspoonful oregano
1-2 oz (25-50g) tomato paste
2 tablespoonsful vegetable oil
Pinch of paprika
Sea salt and freshly ground black pepper

American
1 large onion, sliced
1 clove garlic, crushed
2 carrots, cut into sticks
2 potatoes, diced
2 cupsful mushrooms, sliced
3 sticks celery, chopped
2½ cupsful ripe tomatoes, skinned and
    chopped
1 green pepper, sliced in rings
1 teaspoonful oregano
2½ tablespoonsful tomato paste
2½ tablespoonsful vegetable oil
Pinch of paprika
Sea salt and freshly ground black pepper

Optional:

4 oz (100g) green beans, sliced
4 oz (100g) green peas
4 oz (100g) bean sprouts
Shredded cabbage
Cauliflower florets

¾ cupful green beans, sliced
¾ cupful green peas
2 cupsful bean sprouts
Shredded cabbage
Cauliflower florets

1. *Sauté* the onion and garlic.

2. Add the carrots and potatoes, browning them gently, then add the other ingredients and a little water and mix well.

3. Cover the pan and cook gently for about 30 minutes. Add the optional ingredients just in time for them to cook before serving.

MUSHROOM PANCAKES
IN TOMATO SAUCE

Imperial (Metric)
12 pancakes (basic recipe, page 141)
1 lb (½ kilo) mushrooms, sliced
2 oz (50g) butter
1 small onion, diced finely
2 tablespoonsful tomato paste
Pinch of raw cane sugar
Sea salt and freshly ground black pepper
Tabasco sauce (optional) and marjoram

American
12 pancakes (basic recipe, page 141)
8 cupsful mushrooms, sliced
¼ cupful butter
1 small onion, diced finely
2½ tablespoonsful tomato paste
Pinch of raw cane sugar
Sea salt and freshly ground black pepper
Tabasco sauce (optional) and marjoram

1. *Sauté* the onion in a little vegetable oil or butter, add the tomatoes and seasonings (pepper, salt and sugar). Cook but do not brown the onions.

2. Add the tomato paste and up to ½ pint of water. Cover and simmer for 5-10 minutes.

3. Set aside to cool a little, then blend or sieve. A little *Tabasco* sauce may be added if liked.

4. *Sauté* the mushrooms in the butter and season them with salt, pepper and marjoram.

5. Roll the mushrooms up in the pancakes, place them in a shallow dish and cover them with the sauce. Chopped parsley may be used to garnish the dish.

PANCAKE OMELETTE

Imperial (Metric)
2 eggs
2 tablespoonsful water
Butter or vegetable oil
Sea salt and freshly ground black pepper

American
2 eggs
2½ tablespoonsful water
Butter or vegetable oil
Sea salt and freshly ground black pepper

1. Heat a little butter or oil in a small flat pan.

2. Beat together the eggs, water and seasoning and pour the mixture into the heated pan, cooking until golden underneath.

3. Flip the pancake over to cook lightly on the other side, or leave it slightly moist and runny if preferred.

4. Roll up like a pancake and serve—this may be filled with any steamed or *sautéed* vegetables.

PANCAKES: BASIC RECIPE

Imperial (Metric)
4 oz (100g) wholemeal flour
2 large eggs
2 tablespoonsful vegetable oil
Pinch of sea salt
½ pint (¼ litre) slightly warmed milk

American
1 cupful wholemeal flour
2 large eggs
2½ tablespoonsful vegetable oil
Pinch of sea salt
1¼ cupsful slightly warmed milk

1. Combine the ingredients in the order given. Blend the mixture briefly in a blender if you have one, otherwise beat well with a metal spoon.

2. Cook the mixture by the spoonful in a lightly greased pan. (Experiment to perfect the measurement of spoon and pan and the amount of vegetable oil for greasing the pan—the batter should make 12 pancakes.)

3. Flip the pancake over so that both sides are golden and leave the pan easily. (Pancakes may be kept for a few hours before serving if wrapped in greaseproof paper and a tea-towel.)

PAPRIKA 'BEEF'

Imperial (Metric)
1 small packet soya 'beef' chunks, hydrated
2 large onions, diced
1 clove garlic, crushed
3 tablespoonsful vegetable oil
2-3 dessertspoonsful tomato paste
1 medium-sized tin tomatoes
½ teaspoonful raw cane sugar
1-2 small whole onions per person
2-3 potatoes, peeled
1 small carton double or soured cream or
  yogurt
Freshly ground black pepper

American
1 small packet soya 'beef' chunks, hydrated
2 large onions, diced
1 clove garlic, crushed
4 tablespoonsful vegetable oil
2-3 tablespoonsful tomato paste
1 medium-sized tin tomatoes
½ teaspoonful raw cane sugar
1-2 small whole onions per person
2-3 potatoes, peeled
1 small carton double or soured cream or
  yogurt
Freshly ground black pepper

1. Hydrate the soya 'beef' using 1½ cupsful of hot water. Set the tvp aside for about 10 minutes, then drain.

2. *Sauté* the onion and garlic in the oil, then add the tvp and stir well.

3. Add the remaining ingredients and stir gently, then simmer for 20-30 minutes. (This dish tastes particularly good if prepared in advance and left to stand overnight at this stage.)

4. Slice the potatoes thinly and layer them on top of the stew. Cover the pan and cook until the potatoes are soft but keep their shape.

5. Pour over the yogurt or cream, brown under the grill and serve with green beans.

SAMBALS

Sambals are usually served in small bowls to accompany curry dishes and may include any combination of the following:

Tomato wedges
Lemon wedges
Peanuts
Coconut
Raisins
Sultanas
Apples
Bananas
Oranges, sliced
Popadams
Omelette, cut into thin slices, sprinkled with chilli powder

Pineapple
Papaw
Dhall
Diced green and red peppers
Finely chopped spring onions
Pickled walnuts
Preserved ginger
Chutney
Hard-boiled eggs, in wedges
Cucumber slices with black pepper (in yogurt if liked)

Bananas and yogurt are particularly good to offer to anyone who is unused to the strength of your particular curry. Use them to accompany Savoury Vegetable Curry (page 192), Sweet Spicy Curry (page 144) and Potato and Cauliflower Curry (page 38).

SATURDAY NIGHT SPECIAL

Imperial (Metric)	American
1 onion, diced	1 onion, diced
1 clove garlic, crushed	1 clove garlic, crushed
¾ lb (350g) brown rice, washed	1½ cupsful brown rice, washed
1 large aubergine, diced into large cubes	1 eggplant, diced into large cubes
1 large green pepper, sliced	1 large green pepper, sliced
1 large stick celery, chopped	1 large stick celery, chopped
4 oz (100g) mushrooms, sliced	2 cupsful mushrooms, sliced
2 tablespoonsful sesame seeds	2½ tablespoonsful sesame seeds
1 dessertspoonful caraway seeds	1 tablespoonful caraway seeds
2 tablespoonsful tomato paste	2½ tablespoonsful tomato paste
Approx. ¾ pint (400ml) water	Approx. 1¾ cupsful water
2 tablespoonsful rolled, unpearled barley	2½ tablespoonsful rolled, unpearled barley
1 tablespoonful vegetable oil	1 tablespoonful vegetable oil
Grated cheese to garnish	Grated cheese to garnish

1. *Sauté* the onions and garlic in the oil. Add the rice and stir gently for a few minutes.

2. Mix in the remaining ingredients except the barley.

3. Cover the pan and simmer for about 30 minutes, adding a little water if necessary.

4. Stir in the barley 10 minutes before serving garnished with the grated cheese.

SAVOURY STUFFED MARROW

Imperial (Metric)
1 large marrow
1 small packet tvp 'minced meat'
3 onions, finely diced
2 cloves garlic
2 tablespoonsful vegetable oil
3 tablespoonsful tomato paste
Pinch of rosemary and oregano
Sea salt and freshly ground black pepper

American
1 summer squash
1 small packet tvp 'minced meat'
3 onions, finely diced
2 cloves garlic
2½ tablespoonsful vegetable oil
4 tablespoonsful tomato paste
Pinch of rosemary and oregano
Sea salt and freshly ground black pepper

1. Prepare the marrow by placing it in a shallow ovenproof dish and skewering it four to five times across its length.

2. Bake the marrow for about 20 minutes at 350°F/180°C (Gas Mark 4).

3. When cool, remove the skewers and cut the marrow in half lengthways. Scoop out the seeds, dry the case with kitchen paper and sprinkle the marrow lightly with salt and pepper.

4. *Sauté* the onions and garlic in the oil, add the tvp and stir well.

5. Mix in the remaining ingredients with 1¼ pints (650ml) hot water. Stir again, then simmer gently for 30 minutes to a dry consistency.

6. Pile the mixture into the marrow case and garnish with tomato slices. Bake for a further 20 minutes until sizzling.

SWEET CORN CASSEROLE

Imperial (Metric)
3 large fresh cobs corn, kernels removed or
1 medium-sized tin sweet corn (whole kernels)
1 large onion, diced
2-3 large red tomatoes
2-3 oz (50-75g) cooked brown rice or
 wholemeal noodles
1 tablespoonful tomato paste or
1 teaspoonful *Marmite*
Pinch of oregano or other herbs
Freshly ground black pepper

American
3 large fresh cobs corn, kernels removed or
1 medium-sized tin sweet corn (whole kernels)
1 large onion, diced
2-3 large red tomatoes
1-1½ cupsful cooked brown rice or wholemeal
 noodles
1 tablespoonful tomato paste or
1 teaspoonful *Marmite*
Pinch of oregano or other herbs
Freshly ground black pepper

1. Mix all the ingredients together well and place the mixture in a casserole.

2. Bake in a moderate oven at 350°F/180°C (Gas Mark 4) for 30 minutes. Serve with triangles of hot buttered toast.

SWEET SPICY CURRY

Basic Sauce:

Imperial (Metric)	*American*
5 oz (150g) tomato paste	Approx. 6 tablespoonsful tomato paste
½ pint (¼ litre) water	1¼ cupsful water
2 cloves garlic, crushed	2 cloves garlic, crushed
1 tablespoonful raw cane sugar	1 tablespoonful raw cane sugar
10 cloves (whole)	10 cloves (whole)
1 teaspoonful sea salt	1 teaspoonful sea salt
2 tablespoonsful cider vinegar	2½ tablespoonsful cider vinegar
½ teaspoonful turmeric	½ teaspoonful turmeric
½-1 teaspoonful cinnamon	½-1 teaspoonful cinnamon
2 tablespoonsful *Holbrook's* Worcester sauce	2½ tablespoonsful *Holbrook's* Worcester sauce
½ teaspoonful ground cardamom	½ teaspoonful ground cardamom
½ teaspoonful paprika	½ teaspoonful paprika

1. Combine all the ingredients in a saucepan. Bring to the boil, cover the pan and lower the heat.

2. Simmer for 5 minutes.

Vegetables:

2 large tomatoes, peeled and cut into wedges	2 large tomatoes, peeled and cut into wedges
1-2 large aubergines, unpeeled but sliced	1-2 eggplants, unpeeled but sliced
3 tablespoonsful lemon juice	4 tablespoonsful lemon juice
4 onions, chopped into large rings	4 onions, chopped into large rings
1 large green pepper, cut into strips	1 large green pepper, cut into strips
1 dessertspoonful sea salt	1 tablespoonful sea salt
2 teaspoonsful turmeric	2 teaspoonsful turmeric
Vegetable oil for frying	Vegetable oil for frying

1. Blanch the aubergine in water and lemon juice. Leave to stand for 5 minutes before draining and sprinkling with the salt and turmeric.

2. Deep-fry the aubergine slices in the oil for 2 minutes then drain and add them, with the other vegetables, to the sauce.

3. Simmer for 20 minutes over a very low heat, and serve with brown rice and sambals (page 142).

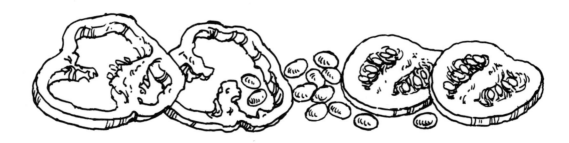

VEGETABLE SAUCE II

(Serves 4-6)

Imperial (Metric)
1 lb (½ kilo) each tomatoes, onions,
  mushrooms, peppers, sliced
1 large clove garlic, crushed
Pinch each of oregano and sweet basil
Olive oil for frying
Freshly ground black pepper to taste

American
1 lb each tomatoes, onions, mushrooms,
  peppers, sliced
1 large clove garlic, crushed
Pinch each of oregano and sweet basil
Olive oil for frying
Freshly ground black pepper to taste

1. *Sauté* the onions and garlic in the oil. Add the peppers, tomatoes and finally the sliced or whole mushrooms. (It is important that the vegetables are sliced into largish pieces so that they retain their shape.)

2. Season generously, cover the pan and simmer for about 30 minutes. (If possible, leave a little longer over a very low heat to let the flavours mingle.)

3. Serve over wholemeal spaghetti with cashew nuts, grated cheese and a green salad as accompaniments. This is also a useful sauce for Lasagne (page 138).

WALNUT LOAF WITH ORANGE SAUCE

Loaf:

Imperial (Metric)	American
½ lb (¼ kilo) walnuts, freshly ground	2 cupsful walnuts, freshly ground
2 4 oz (100g) tins *Tartex* vegetarian *pâté*	2 4 oz (100g) tins *Tartex* vegetarian *pâté*
½ lb (¼ kilo) fresh wholemeal breadcrumbs	6 cupsful fresh wholemeal breadcrumbs
2 large onions, diced finely	2 large onions, diced finely
2 eggs	2 eggs
3 tablespoonsful vegetable oil	4 tablespoonsful vegetable oil
6-8 halved walnuts to garnish	6-8 halved walnuts to garnish
Pinch of basil	Pinch of basil
Rind and flesh of 2 oranges	Rind and flesh of 2 oranges
Sea salt and freshly ground black pepper	Sea salt and freshly ground black pepper

1. *Sauté* the onions in the oil and then set them aside to cool slightly.

2. Prepare the oranges, grating the peel and chopping the flesh.

3. Combine all the ingredients thoroughly and spoon the mixture into a loaf tin lined with greased brown paper. Garnish with the walnut halves.

4. Bake for 40 minutes at 350°F/180°C (Gas Mark 4) and garnish again with slices of orange and sprigs of watercress before serving.

Sauce:

Imperial (Metric)	American
2 tablespoonsful cornflour	2½ tablespoonsful cornflour
1-2 tablespoonsful vegetable oil	1-2 tablespoonsful vegetable oil
1 vegetable stock cube, dissolved in a little water	1 vegetable stock cube, dissolved in a little water
½ pint (¼ litre) white wine	1¼ cupsful white wine
Juice of 2-3 oranges	Juice of 2-3 oranges

1. Mix together the cornflour and oil and cook gently for a couple of minutes over a low heat.

2. Remove the pan from the heat and add the orange juice and stock, whisking well.

3. Return the sauce to the heat and gradually add the wine to taste. (This sauce is best if not too thick.) Serve with steamed or roasted vegetables.

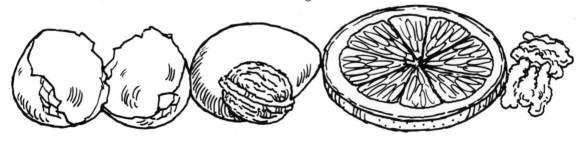

Sweet Dishes

APPLE AND PEAR FRUIT SALAD

Dice and combine 1 red apple, 1 green apple, 1 Comice pear and 1 Conference pear. (Do not peel the fruit.) Add a few blackberries just before serving. Moisten with a little white wine or white grape juice, if necessary.

BANANA AND HAZELNUTS

For each person slice 1 large ripe banana and sprinkle with rum or brandy. Add cream if desired, and top with chopped toasted hazelnuts. Alternatively, layer some chopped bananas and nuts in tall glasses. Top with cream and garnish with a whole toasted nut.

CARAMELLED FRESH FRUIT

Oranges, pears or bananas;
Lemon juice;
Raw cane sugar;
Pinch of garam masala;
Knob of butter.

1. Peel and slice the oranges, peel and halve the pears or peel the bananas.

2. Arrange the fruit in a shallow, buttered ovenproof dish and sprinkle with the remaining ingredients.

3. Bake in a moderate oven at 350°F/180°C (Gas Mark 4) for 15-20 minutes.

CHOCOLATE MOUSSE

For each person use:

Imperial (Metric)
1 oz (25g) dark plain chocolate
1 egg, separated
1-2 tablespoonsful strong black coffee
1 tablespoonful brandy

American
1 square dark plain chocolate
1 egg, separated
2 tablespoonsful strong black coffee
1 tablespoonful brandy

1. Gently melt the chocolate with the coffee in a china or glass bowl over hot water, then remove it from the heat and beat in the egg yolks, one at a time.

2. Whisk the egg whites, preferably by hand, in a stainless steel bowl until they are stiff enough to form peaks but are not too dry.

3. Gradually fold the egg whites into the chocolate and add the brandy.

4. Serve in individual glasses or mousse pots with a bowl of whipped cream. (This dish should be prepared several hours before serving.)

COTTAGE CHEESE AND ALMONDS

Imperial (Metric)
½ lb (¼ kilo) cottage cheese, sieved
4 oz (100g) ground almonds
Few drops of pure vanilla essence
1 teaspoonful honey
2 oz (50g) raisins or sultanas
Juice of 1 lemon
Grated rind of ½ lemon

American
1 cupful cottage cheese, sieved
⅔ cupful ground almonds
Few drops of pure vanilla essence
1 teaspoonful honey
⅔ cupful raisins or sultanas
Juice of 1 lemon
Grated rind of ½ lemon

1. Mix the ingredients together well. Spoon the mixture into individual dishes and leave in a cool place for at least 3-4 hours.

2. Decorate with roasted almonds if liked and cover with clingfilm until ready to serve.

Variation
Soak the dried fruit in 1 tablespoonful of brandy overnight before adding it to the mixture, and omit half the lemon juice.

AUTUMN

Almond-stuffed Marrow (page 132)
Chocolate Mousse (page 148)
Avocado and Mushroom Entrée (page 122)

EGG NOG

For each person use:

Imperial (Metric)
1 egg (yolk only if any digestive problems)
½ pint (¼ litre) milk (skimmed or whole)
Few drops of pure vanilla essence or brandy
Pinch of fresh nutmeg
Clear honey to taste

American
1 egg (yolk only if any digestive problems)
1¼ cupsful milk (skimmed or whole)
Few drops of pure vanilla essence or brandy
Pinch of fresh nutmeg
Clear honey to taste

1. Blend or beat all the ingredients until very fluffy.

2. Pour the mixture into individual glasses and grate nutmeg over the top.

FRUIT MINCE

Imperial (Metric)
1 medium-sized tin crushed pineapple
6 oz (200g) sultanas
6 oz (200g) raisins
3 oz (75g) currants
2 tablespoonsful fresh orange and lemon peel, grated
2 tablespoonsful dried apricots and pears, chopped
2 tablespoonsful dried peaches, finely chopped
1 cooking apple, peeled and grated
½ teaspoonful each cinnamon and nutmeg
1 tablespoonful cornflour
6 tablespoonsful brandy

American
1 medium-sized tin crushed pineapple
1¼ cupsful sultanas
1¼ cupsful raisins
⅓ cupful currants
2½ tablespoonsful fresh orange and lemon peel, grated
2½ tablespoonsful dried apricots and pears, chopped
2½ tablespoonsful dried peaches, finely chopped
1 cooking apple, peeled and grated
½ teaspoonful each cinnamon and nutmeg
1 tablespoonful cornflour
7½ tablespoonsful brandy

1. Combine all the ingredients except for the cornflour and brandy, and stir over a medium heat until the mixture boils.

2. Lower the heat and simmer the fruit for 3 minutes.

3. Blend the cornflour and brandy and mix it into the fruit mixture. Stir until the mixture boils and thickens.

4. Store in clean air-tight jars or use when cool to fill a 9 in. pie case. (This is also good as a hot topping for ice cream or bland puddings.)

AUTUMN

Autumn Glory Soup (page 122)
Walnut Loaf (page 146)
Lasagne with Vegetable Sauce (page 138)

MARMALADE

For this recipe use any citrus fruit, alone or in combinations; for example, grapefruit and orange or lemon and lime.

Imperial (Metric)
2 lb (1 kilo) raw cane sugar (per lb fruit)
2 pints (1 litre) water (per lb fruit)
Juice of 1 lemon (except in lemon and lime marmalade)

American
5 ½ cupsful raw cane sugar (per lb fruit)
5 cupsful water (per lb fruit)
Juice of 1 lemon (except in lemon and lime marmalade)

1. Scrub the fruit gently but thoroughly and dry it well. (Avoid fruit that has been waxed.)

2. Use a potato peeler to remove the peel, finely or coarsely. Use scissors to cut the peel to the preferred width and length.

3. Place the peel and half the water in a pan, cover and simmer it very slowly for about 2 hours to tenderize.

4. Cut the fruit in half. Squeeze the juice and reserve it. Remove the flesh and chop it up. Separate the pith, chop it up and place it in a muslin bag with the pips. Secure the mouth of the bag and place it in the pan, secured to the handle so that it is easy to remove. (The pectin in the pith ensures that the marmalade sets.)

5. Combine all the ingredients except the sugar in a large pan and simmer, uncovered, until the peel is quite soft and the volume has reduced by half—about 2 hours.

6. Remove the bag and add the sugar, stirring to dissolve it.

7. Boil rapidly to setting point—about 15-20 minutes.

8. Skim the top of the marmalade and set it aside for about 30 minutes before pouring into jars.

ORANGE AND LEMON SAUCE

Imperial (Metric)
½ lb (¼ kilo) raw cane sugar
4 oz (100g) butter
2 eggs
Oranges and/or lemons (3 pieces of fruit)

American
1 cupful raw cane sugar
½ cupful butter
2 eggs
Oranges and/or lemons (3 pieces of fruit)

1. Peel the rind and squeeze the juice of the fruit.

2. Place all the ingredients except the eggs in a double saucepan or in a bowl over a saucepan of hot water. Cook gently, stirring the mixture to melt the butter and sugar.

3. Beat the eggs well and add them to the sauce. Continue cooking, stirring constantly until the mixture coats the spoon.

4. When cool, store in sealed jars, preferably in the refrigerator. (This is traditionally a sandwich spread or cake filling, but it is delicious served hot or cold with ice cream. To reheat use a bowl over a saucepan of hot water or a double saucepan.)

PINEAPPLE SLICES

Peel and slice a fresh pineapple fairly thinly. Arrange the slices on a shallow platter and cover with fresh orange juice. Chill before serving.

PORT WINE APPLES

Imperial (Metric)
3 large apples (firm, tart apples are best)
1 oz (25g) butter
2 oz (50g) raw cane sugar
1 teaspoonful cinnamon
¼ pint (150ml) port

American
3 large apples (firm, tart apples are best)
2½ tablespoonsful butter
¼ cupful raw cane sugar
1 teaspoonful cinnamon
¾ cupful port

1. Peel, core and slice the apples.

2. Melt the butter in a deep frying pan. *Sauté* the apples, sprinkle them with the sugar and cinnamon and then add the port.

3. Simmer the apples very gently and serve with whipped cream or custard.

SPICY APPLE OR BANANA PUDDING

Imperial (Metric)	American
2 green apples, peeled cored and sliced or	2 green apples, peeled cored and sliced or
2 bananas, peeled and sliced	2 bananas, peeled and sliced
6 oz (200g) wholemeal flour	1½ cupsful wholemeal flour
3 level teaspoonsful baking powder	3 level teaspoonsful baking powder
2 oz (50g) raw cane sugar	¼ cupful raw cane sugar
1 egg, beaten	1 egg, beaten
2 oz (50g) butter, melted	¼ cupful butter, melted

1. Sift the baking powder, flour and sugar.

2. Add the egg, then the butter, mixing well.

3. Add the fruit, folding it in gently, and place the mixture in a greased ovenproof dish.

Topping:

½ pint (¼ litre) hot water	1¼ cupsful hot water
2 tablespoonsful raw cane sugar	2½ tablespoonsful raw cane sugar
1 oz (25g) butter, melted	2½ tablespoonsful butter, melted
1 teaspoonful mixed spice	1 teaspoonful mixed spice

1. Combine the ingredients thoroughly and pour the mixture over the rest of the pudding.

2. Bake in a moderate oven at 350°F/180°C (Gas Mark 4) for 30 minutes.

TROPICAL FRUIT SALAD

Imperial (Metric)	American
3-4 Chinese gooseberries	3-4 Chinese gooseberries
1 mango	1 mango
1 pawpaw	1 pawpaw
2 bananas	2 bananas
½ large pineapple, chopped	½ large pineapple, chopped
2-4 passion fruit	2-4 passion fruit
2 oz (50g) grated coconut	¾ cupful grated coconut
1 teaspoonful freshly grated root ginger	1 teaspoonful freshly grated root ginger
Juice of 2-3 limes to taste	Juice of 2-3 limes to taste

1. Slice the fruit and combine all the ingredients in an attractive serving dish.

WALNUT AND ORANGE SALAD

To the basic fruit salad (page 108) add some fresh sweet English walnuts, halved. Decorate the dish by arranging finely sliced oranges or segments of ugli or mandarin around the edge.

WINTER

Menu Suggestions

1.
Breakfast
Half a grapefruit
Yogurt (p. 112) with wheatgerm, nuts and seeds

Lunch
Grain Broth (p. 167)
Salad of grated carrots, raisins, parsley and lemon juice
Wholemeal bread and butter

Dinner
Cheese, Potato and Onion Pie (p. 178)
Brussels sprouts and parsnips
or
Salad of Chinese leaves, celery and Brussels sprouts
Fresh fruit

2.
Breakfast
Fresh apples

Lunch
Red Cabbage Salad (p. 173) with yogurt (p. 112)
Eggs and Cheese on Toast (p. 166)

Dinner
Lentil Hot Pot (p. 178)
Green salad
Russian Cream Noela (p. 207)

3.
Breakfast
Stewed diced apricots or peaches with ground almonds and yogurt (p. 112)

Lunch
Sprout and One Salad (p. 173)
Jacket baked potato or brown rice

Dinner
Spinach Tagliatelle in Tomato Sauce (p. 193)
Salad of Chinese leaves in French dressing (p. 171)
Satsumas and bananas in grapefruit juice
or
Lychees and Melon Fruit Salad (p. 204)

4.
Breakfast
Citrus *compote*, boiled egg
or
yogurt (p. 112)

Lunch
Winter Break Salad (p. 174) with wholemeal bread

Dinner
Lentil Roast (p. 179)
or
'Meat' Loaf (p. 181) with steamed carrots and cabbage, roast parsnips and gravy
Cottage Cheese and hazelnuts (p. 202)

5.
Breakfast
Fruit or fruit juice
Wholemeal bread and peanut butter

Lunch
Carrot Soup (p. 165)
Green and Brown Salad (p. 172) with grated cheese

Dinner
Rich Walnut Savoury (p. 189)
Green salad
Grapefruit Dessert (p. 203)

6.
Breakfast
Stewed apples and yogurt (p. 112)

Lunch
Curried Eggs (p. 166)
Salad of celery, Chinese leaves, watercress and tomato dressing
(p. 86) with garlic

Dinner
'Pork' and Vegetable Casserole (p. 186)
or
Mixed Bean Stew with Parsley Dumplings (p. 182)
Dried Fruit Salad (p. 203)

7.
Breakfast
Half a grapefruit or clementines
Wholemeal toast with butter

Lunch
Winter Break Salad (p. 174)
Cheese Loaf (p. 177) served hot or cold

Dinner
Avocado Cream with Mushrooms (p. 163)
Potato Pie (p. 187)
Steamed greens

8.
Breakfast
Yogurt (p. 112) with wheatgerm, fruit and honey

Lunch
Salad of celery, Chinese leaves and red peppers
Wholemeal bread and butter or brown rice

Dinner
Pizza (p. 184)
Green salad with French dressing (p. 171)
Lemon Sorbet (p. 203)

9.
Breakfast
Fresh fruit

Lunch
Swede and Spice Soup (p. 168)
Bean Sprouts and Rice Salad (p. 171)

Dinner
Winter Vegetable Soufflé (p. 195)
Green salad
Cottage Cheese and Apricot Fool (p. 201)

10.
Breakfast
Fresh fruit and yogurt (p. 112)

Lunch
Vegetable Dumpling Soup (p. 169)
Red Cabbage Salad (p. 173)
or
Green and Brown Salad (p. 172)

Dinner
Butter Bean Roast (p. 176)
Roast carrots and parsnips, steamed greens and gravy
Melon wedges

11.
Breakfast
Orange, apple and banana

Lunch
Salad of diced, freshly cooked beetroot, cabbage and yogurt (p. 112)
or
French dressing (p. 171)
Brown rice or wholemeal bread

Dinner
Savoury Bread and Butter Pudding (p. 190)
or
Potato Bake (p. 186)
Steamed vegetables
Baked Apples (p. 198)

12.
Breakfast
Stewed or reconstituted dried fruits with yogurt (p. 112)

Lunch
Lentil Curry Soup (p. 167)
Green salad and grated cheese

Dinner
Carrot and Nut Loaf (p. 177)
Steamed vegetables and gravy
Citrus Fruit Salad (p. 201)

13.
Breakfast
Fresh fruit
Wholemeal toast, honey and tahini

Lunch
Mushroom and Cashew Nut Flan (p. 183)
Green salad

Dinner
Cabbage and Gruyère Savoury (p. 176)
Mashed potatoes and parsley
Date and Cashew Rounds (p. 202)

14.
Breakfast
Stewed apples with yogurt (p. 112) or cream

Lunch
Red Cabbage Casserole (p. 188) with noodles

Dinner
Vegetable Risotto (p. 194)
or
Winter Stew (p. 194)
Green Salad
Cantaloupe and Passion Fruit Salad (p. 201)

Starters

AVOCADO CREAM
WITH MUSHROOMS

Imperial (Metric)
1 ripe avocado
4 oz (100g) mushrooms, finely sliced
¼ teaspoonful honey
1 dessertspoonful oil and lemon dressing
  (page 84)

American
1 ripe avocado
2 cupsful mushrooms, finely sliced
¼ teaspoonful honey
1 tablespoonful oil and lemon dressing
  (page 84)

1. Mash the avocado flesh with the honey and dressing until smooth and creamy.

2. Add the mushrooms together with a small crushed clove of garlic for extra piquancy if liked.

BARLEY SOUP

Imperial (Metric)	American
2 carrots, diced	2 carrots, diced
1 onion, diced	1 onion, diced
2 sticks celery, sliced	2 sticks celery, sliced
2 oz (50g) mushrooms and/or mushroom stalks	1 cupful mushrooms and/or mushroom stalks
2 pints (1 litre) vegetable stock	5 cupsful vegetable stock
3 heaped tablespoonsful whole barley	4 heaped tablespoonsful whole barley
1 small tin tomatoes	1 small tin tomatoes
1 teaspoonful tomato paste	1 teaspoonful tomato paste
Freshly ground black pepper	Freshly ground black pepper

1. Pour the boiling stock over the barley and set it aside for an hour or so.

2. Add the remaining ingredients and simmer gently for 30-40 minutes until the barley is tender but not mushy. Season to taste.

Variation
Use 5-6 tablespoonsful of barley flakes instead of whole grains. Combine all the ingredients and cook the soup for 30 minutes.

CABBAGE SOUP

Imperial (Metric)	American
1 medium-sized winter cabbage, shredded	1 medium-sized winter cabbage, shredded
2 apples, grated	2 apples, grated
1 onion, finely diced	1 onion, finely diced
½ lb (¼ kilo) tomatoes, skinned and finely chopped	2 cupsful tomatoes, skinned and finely chopped
2 pints (1 litre) vegetable stock	5 cupsful vegetable stock
Juice of 1 lemon	Juice of 1 lemon
Sea salt, freshly ground black pepper and raw cane sugar to taste	Sea salt, freshly ground black pepper and raw cane sugar to taste

1. Simmer the vegetables in the stock for 30 minutes.

2. Season to taste with the lemon juice, salt, pepper and sugar.

Variations
The apples may be replaced by 1 cooked beetroot, grated and 1 large carrot, grated.

Serve a little cream in each bowl of soup.

To enrich the cabbage flavour, stir-fry it for a few minutes in 1-2 oz (25-50g) of butter.

CARROT SOUP

Imperial (Metric)
1 lb (½ kilo) carrots, chopped
2 pints (1 litre) water
1 small onion, chopped
1 bay leaf
Pinch each of basil or marjoram and
   mixed spice
Tender cabbage or cauliflower leaves, chopped
Sea salt and freshly ground black pepper

American
1 lb carrots, chopped
5 cupsful water
1 small onion, chopped
1 bay leaf
Pinch each of basil or marjoram and
   mixed spice
Tender cabbage or cauliflower leaves, chopped
Sea salt and freshly ground black pepper

1. Simmer all the ingredients together in a covered saucepan for 30 minutes. Remove the bay leaf.

2. Set aside to cool then sieve or blend the soup to *purée* it.

3. Add a little *Marmite, Vecon,* tomato paste or cream before serving.

CREAM OF TURNIP SOUP

Imperial (Metric)
6 young turnips, sliced
1 onion or leek, diced (optional)
1-2 oz (25-50g) butter
2½ pints (1¼ litres) water
½ teaspoonful sea salt
¼ teaspoonful raw cane sugar
1-2 egg yolks
2 tablespoonsful cream
Freshly ground black pepper

American
6 young turnips, sliced
1 onion or leek, diced (optional)
2½-5 tablespoonsful butter
6¼ cupsful water
½ teaspoonful sea salt
¼ teaspoonful raw cane sugar
1-2 egg yolks
2½ tablespoonsful cream
Freshly ground black pepper

1. *Sauté* the vegetables in the butter for 5 minutes. Season and stir well.

2. Pour on the water and simmer the soup until the turnips are soft.

3. Sieve or blend to a *purée*, return the soup to the saucepan and reheat it.

4. Beat the egg yolks into the cream and whisk this mixture into the soup just before serving. Serve with hot *croûtons* of fried wholemeal bread. Garnish with freshly chopped parsley and grated cheese, if desired.

CURRIED EGGS

Imperial (Metric)
4-6 hard-boiled eggs, quartered
3 tablespoonsful butter
1 onion, diced
1 tablespoonful plain wholemeal flour
1 dessertspoonful curry powder
½ pint (¼ litre) warm milk
Juice of ½ lemon

American
4-6 hard-boiled eggs, quartered
4 tablespoonsful butter
1 onion, diced
1 tablespoonful plain wholemeal flour
1 tablespoonful curry powder
1¼ cupsful warm milk
Juice of ½ lemon

1. *Sauté* the onion in the butter, then add the flour, curry and seasoning. Cook gently for 1 minute.

2. Remove from the heat, gradually add the milk, then cook very gently, stirring constantly to make thick sauce.

3. Mix in the eggs, slowly add the lemon juice and stir gently. Serve on wholemeal toast or with brown rice.

EGGS AND CHEESE ON TOAST

Imperial (Metric)
4 oz (100g) cottage cheese
3-4 oz (75-100g) Cheddar cheese, grated
1 or 2 small eggs, beaten
1 teaspoonful mustard
1 small onion, diced finely
Pinch of sage, sweet basil, rosemary or
    marjoram
Sea salt and freshly ground black pepper

American
½ cupful cottage cheese
1-1½ cupsful Cheddar cheese, grated
1 or 2 small eggs, beaten
1 teaspoonful mustard
1 small onion, diced finely
Pinch of sage, sweet basil, rosemary or
    marjoram
Sea salt and freshly ground black pepper

1. Combine all the ingredients except the eggs.

2. Gradually add the beaten eggs, mixing well. (Do not let the mixture become too soft.)

3. Pile the mixture onto slices of wholemeal bread which has been toasted on one side and brown the egg mixture under the grill. Serve with a salad.

GRAIN BROTH

Imperial (Metric)
1½-2 pints (¾-1 litre) vegetable stock, using
  Vecon, *Tastex*, tomato paste or 1 *Huegli*
  stock cube, if necessary
1 onion, diced
1 carrot, grated
2 sticks celery, chopped
2 tablespoonsful each wheat, rye, oat and
  barley flakes
1 oz (25g) butter
Bouquet garni

American
3¾-5 cupsful vegetable stock, using *Vecon*,
  Tastex, tomato paste or 1 *Huegli* stock cube,
  if necessary
1 onion, diced
1 carrot, grated
2 sticks celery, chopped
2½ tablespoonsful each wheat, rye, oat and
  barley flakes
2½ tablespoonsful butter
Bouquet garni

1. Melt the butter in a saucepan and *sauté* the onion until transparent.

2. Add the carrot and celery and stir for a minute or two.

3. Add the stock and herbs and simmer for 15 minutes.

4. Add the grain flakes and simmer for a further 20-30 minutes.

5. Serve in heavy bowls, garnished with grated Cheddar or other English cheese.

Note: This soup makes a satisfying meal served on its own or followed by a salad.

LENTIL CURRY SOUP

Imperial (Metric)
½ lb (¼ kilo) red lentils
2 large onions, diced
2 cloves garlic, crushed
2-3 tablespoonsful vegetable oil
1 tablespoonful curry powder
1 small potato, diced
3-4 tablespoonsful tomato paste
2½ pints (1¼ litres) water

American
1 cupful red lentils
2 large onions, diced
2 cloves garlic, crushed
3 tablespoonsful vegetable oil
1 tablespoonful curry powder
1 small potato, diced
4 tablespoonsful tomato paste
6¼ cupsful water

1. *Sauté* the onions and garlic in the oil, using a large saucepan. Add the curry powder and cook for about 10 minutes over a low heat, stirring frequently.

2. Add the potato and fry until golden then mix in the remaining ingredients.

3. Simmer gently for about 40 minutes, testing the flavour before removing from the heat. (The soup should be very thick, but the lentils should retain their shape.) Serve on its own or with a salad, but avoid all other starchy food with this meal.

ONION SOUP

Imperial (Metric)
6 medium-sized onions, finely sliced
2½ pints (1¼ litres) water
2 oz (50g) butter
1 dessertspoonful yeast extract or
1 vegetable stock cube
1 tablespoonful freshly chopped parsley
Freshly ground black pepper

American
6 medium-sized onions, finely sliced
6¼ cupsful water
¼ cupful butter
1 tablespoonful yeast extract or
1 vegetable stock cube
1 tablespoonful freshly chopped parsley
Freshly ground black pepper

1. Fry the onions in the butter until brown but not burnt.

2. Pour in the water with the herbs and stock cube or yeast extract.

3. Simmer to reduce the liquid by about one quarter. Add plenty of pepper.

Note: Traditionally this soup has a cheesy crust. To make this place 2 small slices of wholemeal bread in each bowl. Pour in the soup and allow the bread to rise to the surface. Cover the bread with plenty of Gruyère cheese and brown under the grill or in the oven.

Variation
Add dumplings to the soup as it simmers (see Vegetable Dumpling Soup on page 169).

SWEDE AND SPICE SOUP

Imperial (Metric)
1 lb (½ kilo) swede, peeled and roughly diced
1 pint (½ litre) water
2 onions, diced
2-3 tablespoonsful vegetable oil
Approx. 1 teaspoonful fresh root ginger, chopped
Pinch each of cinnamon and fresh nutmeg, grated
1 small carton fresh cream
Fresh parsley, sage or chives to garnish
Sea salt and freshly ground black pepper

American
1 lb swede, peeled and roughly diced
2½ cupsful water
2 onions, diced
3 tablespoonsful vegetable oil
Approx. 1 teaspoonful fresh root ginger, chopped
Pinch each of cinnamon and fresh nutmeg, grated
1 small carton fresh cream
Fresh parsley, sage or chives to garnish
Sea salt and freshly ground black pepper

1. *Sauté* the onions in the oil, but do not brown them. Add the swede and continue cooking for 5 minutes, then add the ginger and stir gently.

2. Pour on the water and season with the salt and pepper. Bring to the boil and simmer for 15-20 minutes.

3. Liquidize the mixture, then add the spices and cook for a further 5 minutes.

4. Add the cream just before serving. (Do not allow the soup to boil after the cream has been added.) Serve garnished with fresh parsley, sage or chives.

VEGETABLE DUMPLING SOUP

Imperial (Metric)
1 onion, diced
2 carrots, diced
1 turnip, diced
3 sticks celery, sliced or
3 tablespoonsful celeriac, grated
1½ pints (¾ litre) vegetable stock
1 green or red pepper, chopped
A little yeast extract

American
1 onion, diced
2 carrots, diced
1 turnip, diced
3 sticks celery, sliced or
4 tablespoonsful celeriac, grated
3¾ cupsful vegetable stock
1 green or red pepper, chopped
A little yeast extract

1. Simmer the vegetables in the stock for 20 minutes.

Dumplings:

6 oz (200g) self-raising wholemeal flour
3 oz (75g) butter or vegetable fat
¼ pint (150ml) milk or water
2 oz (50g) carrot and onion, finely grated
    and mixed
Wheatgerm or bran

1½ cupsful self-raising wholemeal flour
⅓ cupful butter or vegetable fat
¾ cupful milk or water
⅓ cupful carrot and onion, finely grated
    and mixed
Wheatgerm or bran

1. Rub the fat into the sifted dry ingredients and mix to a stiff dough with the liquid.

2. Shape the dough into small balls and roll them in the wheatgerm or bran. Chill.

3. Place the dumplings in the boiling soup and cook them for 20 minutes with the lid secure.

Note: Dumplings go well with any clear soup. Flavour them to suit the soup: for example, onion and parsley or cheese dumplings with Onion Soup (page 168).

WINTER SOUP

Imperial (Metric)
1-2 carrots, chopped
1 parsnip, chopped
1 turnip, chopped
1 swede, chopped
1 large onion, diced
1 large clove garlic, crushed
1 stick celery, sliced
1 teaspoonful kelp
Pinch each of thyme, basil, parsley, sage
   (fresh if possible)
Freshly ground black pepper

American
1-2 carrots, chopped
1 parsnip, chopped
1 turnip, chopped
1 swede, chopped
1 large onion, diced
1 large clove garlic, crushed
1 stick celery, sliced
1 teaspoonful kelp
Pinch each of thyme, basil, parsley, sage
   (fresh if possible)
Freshly ground black pepper

1. Cover the vegetables with vegetable stock or cold water.

2. Add the kelp and simmer for 20-30 minutes.

3. Season with the fresh herbs and black pepper just before serving.

Salads and Salad Dressings

BEAN SPROUTS AND RICE SALAD

Imperial (Metric)
½ lb (¼ kilo) fresh young bean sprouts—
   preferably mung and brown lentil
4 oz (100g) brown rice, cooked and cooled

American
4 cupsful fresh young bean sprouts—
   preferably mung and brown lentil
½ cupful brown rice, cooked and cooled

1. Combine the rice and bean sprouts with an oil and vinegar or tomato dressing (pages 30 and 86).

FRENCH DRESSING

Imperial (Metric)
3 tablespoonsful vegetable oil
1 tablespoonful cider vinegar
¼ teaspoonful honey
1 teaspoonful French mustard
1 clove garlic, crushed (optional)
1 tablespoonful fresh herbs, chopped (optional)
Freshly ground black pepper

American
3½ tablespoonsful vegetable oil
1 tablespoonful cider vinegar
¼ teaspoonful honey
1 teaspoonful French mustard
1 clove garlic, crushed (optional)
1 tablespoonful fresh herbs, chopped (optional)
Freshly ground black pepper

1. Combine the ingredients thoroughly.

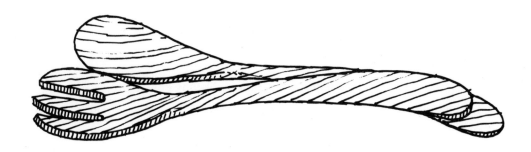

GREEN AND BROWN SALAD

Imperial (Metric)
½ lb (¼ kilo) fresh young spinach leaves
½ lb (½ kilo) button mushrooms, sliced
1 shallot, chopped into rings
1 tablespoonful sesame seeds

American
½ lb fresh young spinach leaves
4 cupsful button mushrooms, sliced
1 shallot, chopped into rings
1 tablespoonful sesame seeds

1. Soak the leaves for a few minutes, shake them well and leave them to drain.

2. Tear the leaves into bite-sized pieces.

3. Combine all the ingredients in a salad bowl and toss in either a yogurt or oil and vinegar dressing (pages 32 and 30).

MAYONNAISE

Imperial (Metric)
2½ pints (1¼ litres) olive oil
2 egg yolks
½ teaspoonful dry mustard
1 clove garlic, crushed
1 teaspoonful lemon juice
2-3 tablespoonsful cider vinegar
Sea salt and freshly ground black pepper
Raw cane sugar to taste

American
6¼ cupsful olive oil
2 egg yolks
½ teaspoonful dry mustard
1 clove garlic, crushed
1 teaspoonful lemon juice
3 tablespoonsful cider vinegar
Sea salt and freshly ground black pepper
Raw cane sugar to taste

1. Whisk the eggs, lemon juice and seasonings.

2. Add 2 tablespoonsful of oil, 2-3 drops at a time, whisking constantly.

3. Add 1 tablespoonful of vinegar and continue to mix in the oil gradually, occasionally adding a little vinegar to prevent over-thickening.

RED CABBAGE SALAD

Imperial (Metric)
1 small red cabbage, finely sliced
1 large onion, sliced into rings
1-2 large apples, diced

American
1 small red cabbage, finely sliced
1 large onion, sliced into rings
1-2 large apples, diced

1. Toss the ingredients in a cole-slaw dressing (page 128) or in plain yogurt.

SPROUT AND ONE SALAD

For this salad, fresh home-sprouted seeds may be combined with any one other fruit or vegetable. For example: tomato, peppers, watercress, mushrooms, avocados, citrus fruit, apples or pears. Choose the dressing to suit the varied vegetables.

In any green salad, sprouts may be used instead of lettuce or cabbage. Seven-day alfalfa sprouts are especially good. (See the instructions in the Introduction for sprouting seeds at home.)

WINTER BREAK SALAD

Imperial (Metric)
½-¾ lb (225-350g) carrots, coarsely grated
1 large onion, finely diced
4 oz (100g) strong Cheddar cheese,
   (e.g. Farmhouse or Black Wax), grated

American
½-¾ lb carrots, coarsely grated
1 large onion, finely diced
1 cupful strong Cheddar cheese,
   (e.g. Farmhouse or Black Wax), grated

1. Toss all the ingredients in French dressing (page 171).

Variations
½ medium-sized swede, grated finely
and
1 medium-sized turnip, grated coarsely

or

10 oz (300g) cooked brown rice
and
2 oz (50g) extra cheese

Either of these variations may be added to the basic salad ingredients.

Savoury Dishes

BAKED BEANS IN TOMATO SAUCE

Imperial (Metric)
1 lb (½ kilo) haricot beans, soaked for 6-12
   hours
1 tablespoonful molasses
1 dessertspoonful dry mustard
2 tablespoonsful cider vinegar
5-6 tablespoonsful tomato paste
Sea salt and freshly ground black pepper

American
2 cupsful navy beans, soaked for 6-12
   hours
1 tablespoonful molasses
1 tablespoonful dry mustard
2½ tablespoonsful cider vinegar
7 tablespoonsful tomato paste
Sea salt and freshly ground black pepper

1.   Boil the beans for at least 10 minutes and then simmer until just tender.

2.   Combine all the ingredients with ½-¾ pint (275-400ml) water in a heavy covered pot.

3.   Cook very slowly in the oven for 4 hours at 225°F/110°C (Gas Mark ¼).

BUTTER BEAN ROAST

Imperial (Metric)	American
½ lb (¼ kilo) butter beans, soaked	1 cupful navy beans, soaked
3 large onions, diced	3 large onions, diced
2 oz (50g) butter	¼ cupful butter
1 teaspoonful sage	1 teaspoonful sage
1 egg	1 egg
2 oz (50g) ground nuts	½ cupful ground nuts
1 oz (25g) soft wholemeal breadcrumbs	⅔ cupful soft wholemeal breadcrumbs
1 dessertspoonful yeast extract	1 tablespoonful yeast extract
2 tablespoonsful vegetable oil	2½ tablespoonsful vegetable oil

1. Cook the butter beans by boiling them for 10 minutes and then simmering them until tender.

2. Drain and mash the beans and *sauté* the onions in the oil over a low heat.

3. Mix all the ingredients together and spoon into a well greased baking dish.

4. Bake for 30 minutes at 350°F/180°C (Gas Mark 4).

CABBAGE AND GRUYÈRE SAVOURY

Imperial (Metric)	American
1 small cabbage, shredded very finely	1 small cabbage, shredded very finely
1 onion, diced finely	1 onion, diced finely
2 oz (50g) butter	¼ cupful butter
3 eggs	3 eggs
½ pint (¼ litre) milk or	1¼ cupsful milk or
¼ pint (150ml) each milk and cream	¾ cupful milk and cream
6 oz (200g) Gruyère cheese, grated finely	1½ cupsful Gruyère cheese, grated finely
2 oz (50g) Parmesan cheese, grated finely	½ cupful Parmesan cheese, grated finely
1 tablespoonful poppy seeds and/or wholemeal breadcrumbs	1 tablespoonful poppy seeds and/or wholemeal breadcrumbs
Pinch of nutmeg, freshly grated	Pinch of nutmeg, freshly grated
Freshly ground black pepper	Freshly ground black pepper

1. Place the cabbage in a colander and rinse well. Set aside to drain.

2. *Sauté* the onion in the butter using a large saucepan. Add the cabbage, stir well and cover. Cook very gently until the cabbage is just tender—about 20-30 minutes. Drain and allow to cool slightly.

3. Meanwhile, prepare the 'custard' by combining the eggs, seasonings, liquid and cheeses and beating well.

4. Combine the cabbage with the custard and pour the mixture into a greased ovenproof dish.

5. Sprinkle with the seeds and/or breadcrumbs and bake gently at 325°F/170°C (Gas Mark 3) for about 30 minutes until the mixture is just set and the top is golden.

Variation
Omit the cream and add ½ pint (¼ litre) of milk with 4 oz (100g) of Gruyère and 4 oz (100g) of cream or cottage cheese (sieved) to the custard mixture. This mixture also serves as a good quiche filling. It is rather rich so serve it with a simple green salad.

CARROT AND NUT LOAF

Imperial (Metric)	*American*
2 onions, diced	2 onions, diced
1 tablespoonful vegetable oil	1 tablespoonful vegetable oil
2 medium-sized carrots, coarsely grated	2 medium-sized carrots, coarsely grated
2 oz (50g) wholemeal breadcrumbs	1½ cupsful wholemeal breadcrumbs
1 tablespoonful parsley, chopped	1 tablespoonful parsley, chopped
½ lb (¼ kilo) walnuts or peanuts, ground	2 cupsful walnuts or peanuts, ground
2 eggs, beaten	2 eggs, beaten
¼ pint (150ml) vegetable or *Marmite* stock	¾ cupful vegetable or *Marmite* stock

1. *Sauté* the onions in oil until transparent, then combine them with the other ingredients.

2. Spoon the mixture into a greased loaf tin. Level the top and dot with butter, then bake for 1 hour at 325°F/170°C (Gas Mark 3).

CHEESE LOAF

Imperial (Metric)	*American*
4 oz (100g) fresh wholemeal breadcrumbs	2½ cupsful fresh wholemeal breadcrumbs
4 oz (100g) mature Cheddar cheese, grated	1½ cupsful mature Cheddar cheese, grated
2 tablespoonsful Parmesan cheese, grated	2½ tablespoonsful Parmesan cheese, grated
1 teaspoonful dry mustard	1 teaspoonful dry mustard
1 large onion, diced	1 large onion, diced
1 tablespoonful vegetable oil	1 tablespoonful vegetable oil
2 tablespoonsful fresh parsley, chopped	2½ tablespoonsful fresh parsley, chopped
1-2 eggs, lightly beaten	1-2 eggs, lightly beaten
Pinch of cayenne pepper	Pinch of cayenne pepper

1. Soften the onion in the oil over a low heat.

2. Combine all the ingredients (1 oz of breadcrumbs may be replaced by 1 oz of bran) and spoon the mixture into a loaf tin or shallow ovenproof dish.

3. Sprinkle with Parmesan cheese and bake for 30 minutes at 350°F/180°C (Gas Mark 4).

CHEESE, POTATO AND ONION PIE

Imperial (Metric)
1 lb (½ kilo) potatoes, boiled and sliced or
    mashed
6 oz (200g) grated cheese
2 large onions, sliced into rings
1 clove garlic, crushed
1-2 tablespoonsful vegetable oil
Pinch each of nutmeg, thyme and cayenne

American
1 lb potatoes, boiled and sliced or
    mashed
1 cupful grated cheese
2 large onions, sliced into rings
1 clove garlic, crushed
1-2 tablespoonsful vegetable oil
Pinch each of nutmeg, thyme and cayenne

1. If you are using mashed potatoes for this dish, mix in one or more of the following ingredients: 2 tablespoonsful of yogurt or cottage cheese, a little cream or butter, 1-2 beaten eggs, sea salt and freshly ground black pepper.

2. *Sauté* the onion rings and garlic in the vegetable oil.

3. Arrange the potatoes, cheese and onions in repeated layers in a buttered ovenproof dish, ending with potato. Season each layer with the nutmeg, thyme and cayenne pepper.

4. Decorate the pie with mushrooms dotted with butter if liked, or with slices of tomato.

5. Brown well in a moderate oven at 350°F/180°C (Gas Mark 4) for 20-30 minutes.

LENTIL HOT POT

Imperial (Metric)
1 lb (½ kilo) brown lentils, washed and soaked
    for 4-5 hours in hot water
1 lb (½ kilo) onions, diced
1 lb (½ kilo) carrots, chopped into sticks
3 sticks celery, chopped
1 lb (½ kilo) green beans, sliced or
1 lb (½ kilo) spinach, shredded
1 oz (25g) parsley, chopped
1 dessertspoonful dried thyme
1-2 tablespoonsful *Marmite*
Freshly ground black pepper

American
2 cupsful brown lentils, washed and soaked for
    4-5 hours in hot water
1 lb onions, diced
1 lb carrots, chopped into sticks
3 sticks celery, chopped
1 lb green beans, sliced or
1 lb spinach, shredded
½ cupful parsley, chopped
1 tablespoonful dried thyme
1-2 tablespoonsful *Marmite*
Freshly ground black pepper

1. Simmer the soaked lentils until about half cooked—so that they are still crisp.

2. Add the other ingredients and simmer for 1 hour over a low heat.

LENTIL ROAST

Imperial (Metric)	American
2 onions, diced	2 onions, diced
1 tablespoonful vegetable oil	1 tablespoonful vegetable oil
½ pint (¼ litre) vegetable or *Marmite* stock	1¼ cupsful vegetable or *Marmite* stock
½ lb (¼ kilo) lentils	1 cupful lentils
2 oz (50g) Cheddar cheese, grated or	⅔ cupful Cheddar cheese, grated or
Pinch of marjoram	Pinch of marjoram
1-2 oz (25-50g) wholemeal breadcrumbs	¾-1½ cupsful wholemeal breadcrumbs

1. *Sauté* the onions in the oil until transparent.

2. Add the stock and lentils to the pan, cover and simmer for 10 minutes or until just tender.

3. Add the cheese and breadcrumbs, mix well and turn into a greased loaf tin.

4. Bake at 325°F/170°C (Gas Mark 3) for 1 hour. Serve with a gravy made with a little vegetable oil mixed with a little rice flour. Cook the roux for a few minutes, then add about ½ pint vegetable stock and flavour with *Marmite* and freshly ground black pepper. Stir until smooth and thick.

Variation
Yellow split peas, soaked overnight, may be used instead of lentils.

LENTIL SHEPHERD'S PIE

Imperial (Metric)
½ lb (¼ kilo) lentils or
4 oz (100g) each lentils and split peas
1 large onion, diced
1 large carrot, diced
1 stick celery, chopped
4-6 oz (100-200g) mushrooms, chopped
4 tablespoonsful butter
1 teaspoonful vegetable oil
1 bay leaf
½ teaspoonful herbs
1 tablespoonful tomato *purée*
1 teaspoonful yeast extract
Freshly ground black pepper to taste

American
1 cupful lentils or
½ cupful each lentils and split peas
1 large onion, diced
1 large carrot, diced
1 stick celery, chopped
2-3 cupsful mushrooms, chopped
5 tablespoonsful butter
1 teaspoonful vegetable oil
1 bay leaf
½ teaspoonful herbs
1 tablespoonful tomato *purée*
1 teaspoonful yeast extract
Freshly ground black pepper to taste

1. Wash and drain the lentils, then simmer them in fresh water until tender and drain any excess water.

2. *Sauté* all the vegetables in the fat until tender—about 15 minutes.

3. Mix in the remaining ingredients and the lentils and turn the mixture into a greased ovenproof dish.

Topping:

1½ lb (¾ kilo) potatoes, boiled for mashing
1 oz (25g) butter
4 oz (100g) cottage cheese, sieved
Pinch of nutmeg
Sea salt and freshly ground black pepper
Cooking water to moisten if necessary

1½ lb potatoes, boiled for mashing
2½ tablespoonsful butter
½ cupful cottage cheese, sieved
Pinch of nutmeg
Sea salt and freshly ground black pepper
Cooking water to moisten if necessary

1. Combine all the ingredients and beat until smooth and creamy. Spread this over the lentil mixture and dot with butter or grated cheese.

2. Bake for 30-40 minutes at 350°F/180°C (Gas Mark 4) to brown the top. Serve with fresh steamed beans or courgettes and gravy.

MACARONI CHEESE

Imperial (Metric)
½-¾ lb (225-350g) macaroni, well cooked but
  still 'chewy'
Approx. 1 pint (½ litre) cheese sauce (page 136)
Parmesan cheese to garnish

American
4½ cupsful macaroni, well cooked but still
  'chewy'
Approx. 2½ cupsful cheese sauce (page 136)
Parmesan cheese to garnish

1. Combine the ingredients in an ovenproof dish, top with the grated Parmesan cheese and brown gently under the grill. (Slices of tomato beneath the cheese topping add piquancy to this dish.)

'MEAT' LOAF

Imperial (Metric)
1 cupful tvp, hydrated and drained
2 oz (50g) soft wholemeal breadcrumbs
2 onions, diced
1-2 cloves garlic, crushed
2 tablespoonsful vegetable oil
1 tablespoonful *Tastex* or *Vecon* or
2 tablespoonsful tomato paste
4 oz (100g) ground almonds
4 oz (100g) walnuts, chopped
1 egg, beaten (optional)

American
1¼ cupsful tvp, hydrated and drained
1¼ cupsful soft wholemeal breadcrumbs
2 onions, diced
1-2 cloves garlic, crushed
2½ tablespoonsful vegetable oil
1 tablespoonful *Tastex* or *Vecon* or
2½ tablespoonsful tomato paste
1 cupful ground almonds
1 cupful walnuts, chopped
1 egg, beaten (optional)

1. *Sauté* the onions and garlic in the oil.

2. Mix the *Tastex*, *Vecon* or tomato paste with the tvp and add the remaining ingredients to the onions.

3. Combine both mixtures thoroughly and place in an oiled ovenproof dish.

4. Bake for 30-40 minutes at 375°F/190°C (Gas Mark 5), covering for part of the time if the oven is too hot. Serve with roast potatoes, carrots or parsnips or with steamed vegetables, (diced and placed with a little water in a covered dish in the oven.) This mixture is also good for making rissoles.

MIXED BEAN STEW WITH PARSLEY DUMPLINGS

Imperial (Metric)
½ lb (¼ kilo) mixed beans, soaked and cooked
    for 1 hour
4 oz (100g) green split peas, soaked and cooked
    for 1 hour
2 oz (50g) butter
1 tablespoonful vegetable oil
2 leeks, chopped
2-3 carrots, chopped
2 sticks celery, chopped
1 onion, sliced
2 courgettes, sliced
2 tomatoes, sliced
4 oz (100g) mushrooms, chopped
2 tablespoonsful tomato *purée*
1 tablespoonful fine oatmeal
1 vegetable stock cube
1½ pints (¾ litre) water
1 tablespoonful yeast extract
¼ teaspoonful each mace, mint and coriander
1 tablespoonful fresh parsley, chopped

American
1 cupful mixed beans, soaked and cooked for
    1 hour
½ cupful green split peas, soaked and cooked
    for 1 hour
¼ cupful butter
1 tablespoonful vegetable oil
2 leeks, chopped
2-3 carrots, chopped
2 sticks celery, chopped
1 onion, sliced
2 zucchini, sliced
2 tomatoes, sliced
2 cupsful mushrooms, chopped
2½ tablespoonsful tomato *purée*
1 tablespoonful fine oatmeal
1 vegetable stock cube
3¾ cupsful water
1 tablespoonful yeast extract
¼ teaspoonful each mace, mint and coriander
1 tablespoonful fresh parsley, chopped

1. *Sauté* all the vegetables for 15 minutes. Stir in the oatmeal, cook for 1 minute and then add all the ingredients except for the yeast extract and parsley.

2. Cook for 1 hour.

Dumplings:

4 oz (100g) wholemeal flour, self-raising
2 oz (50g) butter or polyunsaturated margarine
1 tablespoonful fresh parsley, chopped

1 cupful wholemeal flour, self-raising
¼ cupful butter or polyunsaturated margarine
1 tablespoonful fresh parsley, chopped

1. Rub the fat into the flour. Add the parsley and enough water to mix to a soft dough.

2. Divide the dough into eight pieces. Steam the dumplings, covered, over a pan of boiling water for 15 minutes.

3. Add the yeast extract and parsley to the stew, place the dumplings on top and simmer, covered, for 30 minutes.

MUSHROOM AND CASHEW NUT FLAN

Pastry:

Imperial (Metric)
6 oz (200g) wholemeal flour
3 oz (75g) vegetable shortening or
  butter
1 egg yolk
Tepid water to mix

American
1½ cupsful wholemeal flour
7½ tablespoonsful vegetable shortening or
  butter
1 egg yolk
Tepid water to mix

1. Rub the fat into the flour, and the egg yolk and enough water to make a pliable dough.

2. Roll out the pastry to fit the case and bake blind for 20 minutes at 400°F/200°C (Gas Mark 6), pricking the bottom of the pastry case beforehand.

Filling:

Imperial (Metric)
2-3 oz (50-75g) mushrooms, chopped
5 oz (150g) cashew nuts, broken
1 small onion, finely chopped
1 tablespoonful butter
1½ pints (¾ litre) hot water
1 teaspoonful yeast extract
¼ pint (150ml) apple juice
Pinch of sage
2 teaspoonsful sago or wholemeal flour
Sea salt and freshly ground black pepper

American
1-1½ cupsful mushrooms, chopped
1¼ cupsful cashew nuts, broken
1 small onion, finely chopped
1 tablespoonful butter
3¾ cupsful hot water
1 teaspoonful yeast extract
¾ cupful apple juice
Pinch of sage
2 teaspoonsful sago or wholemeal flour
Sea salt and freshly ground black pepper

1. Melt the butter in a pan, and cook the onion for half a minute over a gentle heat.

2. Add the mushrooms and flour or sago and stir well.

3. Mix in the remaining ingredients and allow to simmer for 15 minutes before pouring it into the pastry case. Serve warm or cold with a salad.

PIZZA

Base:

Imperial (Metric)	American
½ lb (¼ kilo) wholemeal flour	2 cupsful wholemeal flour
½ teaspoonful each sea salt and raw cane sugar	½ teaspoonful each sea salt and raw cane sugar
¼ pint (150ml) water	¾ cupful water
1 teaspoonful yeast	1 teaspoonful yeast

1. Proceed as for bread: basic recipe (page 211). Before proving the dough, wrap it in well oiled plastic and leave in a cool place until ½-1 hour before use.

2. Oil the pizza plate and gently stretch the dough to fit the shape. (This quantity of dough makes two 8 in. pizzas or one large pizza.)

Topping:

Imperial (Metric)	American
2-3 tablespoonsful tomato paste	3 tablespoonsful tomato paste
1 large onion, diced	1 large onion, diced
1 clove garlic, crushed	1 clove garlic, crushed
1 green pepper, sliced	1 green pepper, sliced
¼-½ lb (100-225g) mushrooms, sliced	2-4 cupsful mushrooms, sliced
1-2 tomatoes, sliced thickly	1-2 tomatoes, sliced thickly
Pinch of Italian seasoning	Pinch of Italian seasoning
Sea salt and freshly ground black pepper	Sea salt and freshly ground black pepper
Strong Cheddar cheese, grated or mozzarella cheese, crumbled	Strong Cheddar cheese, grated or mozzarella cheese, crumbled
Olives and mushrooms to garnish	Olives and mushrooms to garnish

1. Spread the tomato paste over the dough and sprinkle thoroughly with pepper and salt and Italian seasoning.

2. *Sauté* the onion, garlic, pepper and mushrooms and arrange this mixture on the dough, topping with a layer of tomato slices.

3. Cover with the grated cheese and decorate with the sliced mushrooms or olives if liked.

4. Bake for 30-45 minutes at 425°F/220°C (Gas Mark 7). (This pizza is much more satisfying than some as the proportion of filling to bread is much higher. It makes a substantial meal served with a simple green salad.)

Note: Sieved cottage cheese may replace some of the grated Cheddar or mozzarella cheese. Combine the two before topping with the vegetables. A quick pizza is made by using thick slices of wholemeal bread instead of dough and proceeding as above. This is useful as a lunchtime dish for children.

WINTER

Winter Vegetable Soufflé (page 195)
Lentil Shepherd's Pie (page 180)
Baked Apples (page 198)

'PORK' AND VEGETABLE CASSEROLE

Imperial (Metric)	American
1 small packet soya 'pork' chunks, hydrated	1 small packet soya 'pork' chunks, hydrated
1 large onion, diced	1 large onion, diced
2 tablespoonsful vegetable oil	2½ tablespoonsful vegetable oil
1 dessertspoonful *Marmite* or *Tastex*	1 tablespoonful *Marmite* or *Tastex*
1 tablespoonful tomato paste	1 tablespoonful tomato paste
1 tablespoonful dry sherry	1 tablespoonful dry sherry
Pinch of thyme	Pinch of thyme
Small whole carrots and onions	Small whole carrots and onions
Large pieces marrow, unpeeled	Large pieces summer squash, unpeeled
Large pieces parsnip	Large pieces parsnip
Parsley to garnish	Parsley to garnish
Sea salt and freshly ground black pepper	Sea salt and freshly ground black pepper

1. *Sauté* the onion in the oil, then add the soya chunks.

2. Mix in the flavourings with ¼ pint (150ml) water and stir well.

3. Add the carrots, onions and parsnips, cover the pan and simmer for 30 minutes.

4. Place the marrow slices on top, cover the pan again and cook gently until the marrow is tender.

5. Sprinkle with chopped parsley and serve with steamed potatoes.

POTATO BAKE

Imperial (Metric)	American
2 lb (1 kilo) potatoes, boiled	2 lb potatoes, boiled
2 eggs	2 eggs
½ lb (¼ kilo) cottage cheese, sieved	1 cupful cottage cheese, sieved
1-2 oz (25-50g) fresh parsley, chopped	¾ cupful fresh parsley, chopped
Pinch of freshly grated nutmeg	Pinch of freshly grated nutmeg
2-3 tablespoonsful strong Cheddar cheese (optional)	3 tablespoonsful strong Cheddar cheese (optional)
Sea salt and freshly ground black pepper	Sea salt and freshly ground black pepper

1. Mash the potatoes with the other ingredients until fluffy.

2. Pile the mixture into a deep, oiled ovenproof dish. Sprinkle with the Cheddar cheese, if liked, and bake at 425°F/220°C (Gas Mark 7) for 20-30 minutes.

POTATO PIE

Base:

Imperial (Metric)	*American*
1-2 large potatoes per person, steamed or boiled	1-2 large potatoes per person, steamed or boiled
3-4 tablespoonsful potato cooking water	4 tablespoonsful potato cooking water
Knob of butter	Knob of butter
Pinch of cayenne pepper or freshly grated nutmeg	Pinch of cayenne pepper or freshly grated nutmeg
Grated cheese to garnish	Grated cheese to garnish
Sea salt and freshly ground black pepper	Sea salt and freshly ground black pepper

1. Oil a deep ovenproof dish and cover the base with half the potato, mashed with the water, butter and seasoning.

2. In the centre place a thick layer of vegetables (see suggestions below), then cover with the rest of the potato.

3. Garnish with grated cheese, nutmeg or cayenne and bake for 20-30 minutes at 350°F/180°C (Gas Mark 4). Serve with a simple salad or green vegetables.

Filling Suggestions

i. ½ lb (¼ kilo) mushrooms, ½ lb (¼ kilo) tomatoes, *sautéed* in lemon juice.

ii. 1 onion, 1 red and 1 green pepper, chopped and *sautéed*.

iii. 2 large grated carrots, *sautéed* with 1 onion and 4 oz (100g) mushrooms or sweet corn.

Variations

i. Add grated Cheddar cheese, lactic or cottage cheese to the potato mash.

ii. Add chopped chives or parsley to the potatoes.

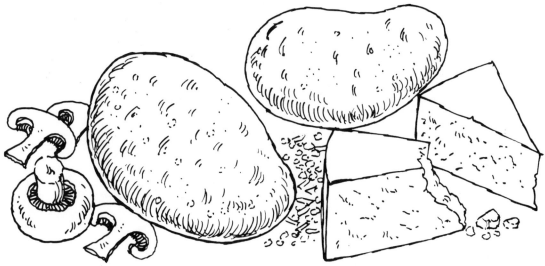

RED CABBAGE CASSEROLE

Imperial (Metric)
1 medium-sized red cabbage, finely shredded
2 cooking apples, chopped
2 large onions, diced
2 tablespoonsful cider vinegar
2 tablespoonsful water
1 teaspoonful light honey
Pinch of sea salt
1 oz (25g) butter
1 oz (25g) wholemeal flour
Fresh parsley to garnish

American
1 medium-sized red cabbage, finely shredded
2 cooking apples, chopped
2 large onions, diced
2 tablespoonsful cider vinegar
2½ tablespoonsful water
1 teaspoonful light honey
Pinch of sea salt
2½ tablespoonsful butter
¼ cupful wholemeal flour
Fresh parsley to garnish

1. Butter a heavy casserole and make several layers of the cabbage, apples and onions.

2. Combine the honey, salt, water and vinegar and stir to dissolve the honey.

3. Pour the liquid over the cabbage mixture, cover and bake for 2 hours at 300°F/150°C (Gas Mark 2).

4. Combine the butter and flour and sprinkle this mixture over the cabbage. Bake uncovered for a further 10 minutes.

Note: Serve this dish with egg noodles and garnish with chopped parsley.

RICH WALNUT SAVOURY

Imperial (Metric)
1 lb (½ kilo) potatoes
1 small onion, finely chopped or
2 tablespoonful parsley, chopped
1 tablespoonful skimmed milk powder
Pinch of nutmeg, freshly grated
3 egg whites, stiffly beaten
6 oz (200g) blue-veined cheese—Stilton,
    Roquefort or Danish Blue
4 oz (100g) cottage cheese
¼ pint (150ml) single cream
3 egg yolks
3 oz (75g) halved walnuts
Sea salt and freshly ground black pepper
Fresh parsley to garnish

American
1 lb potatoes
1 small onion, finely chopped or
2½ tablespoonsful parsley, chopped
1 tablespoonful skimmed milk powder
Pinch of nutmeg, freshly grated
3 egg whites, stiffly beaten
1½ cupsful blue-veined cheese—Stilton,
    Roquefort or Danish Blue
½ cupful cottage cheese
1 cupful single cream
3 egg yolks
¾ cupful halved walnuts
Sea salt and freshly ground black pepper
Fresh parsley to garnish

1. Boil and drain the potatoes, reserving the cooking water.

2. Mash the potatoes and stir in the onion or parsley.

3. Add the butter, skimmed milk powder and enough of the potato water to make a light mash. Beat the mixture well.

4. Fold in the egg whites carefully and place the mixture in a well buttered ovenproof dish.

5. Sieve the cheeses together and add the remaining ingredients, combining well.

6. Pour the mixture over the potato and decorate with the walnut halves.

7. Bake for 30 minutes at 350°F/180°C (Gas Mark 4) until the top is golden. Garnish with sprigs of parsley and serve with a salad.

Note: This cheese mixture also makes a good stuffing for marrows: Parboil the marrow or bake it whole in a moderate oven for 30 minutes. Halve it lengthways and carefully remove all the seeds and pith. Dry the insides with a paper towel and coat them with wholemeal breadcrumbs. Place the marrow in an ovenproof dish and spoon in the cheese mixture. Bake for 30 minutes at 325°F/170°C (Gas Mark 3), then turn up the oven to 375°F/190°C (Gas Mark 5) for 10 minutes.

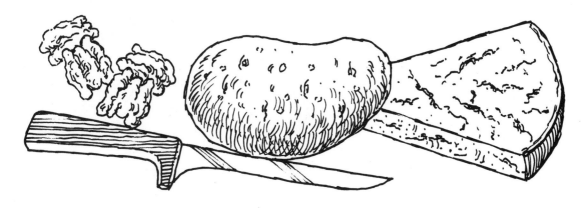

SAVOURY BREAD AND BUTTER PUDDING

Imperial (Metric)
4-6 thick slices wholemeal bread, well buttered
4-6 oz (100-200g) Cheddar, Edam or Swiss
   cheese, grated
2-3 eggs
½-¾ pint (275-400ml) milk or milk and white
   wine
1-2 tablespoonsful parsley, chopped or
Pinch of rosemary or basil

American
4-6 thick slices wholemeal bread, well buttered
1½-2 cupsful Cheddar, Edam or Swiss cheese,
   grated
2-3 eggs
1¼-2 cupsful milk or milk and white
   wine
1-2 tablespoonsful parsley, chopped or
Pinch of rosemary or basil

1. Place the bread and cheese in alternate layers in a deep, oiled ovenproof dish, finishing with a layer of cheese.

2. Pour over half the liquid and leave to soak for ½ hour.

3. Combine the remaining ingredients and beat well before pouring the mixture over the bread and cheese.

4. Bake at 325°F/170°C (Gas Mark 3) for 40 minutes.

WINTER

Gazpacho (page 73)
'Meat' Loaf (page 181)
Rich Christmas Pudding (page 206)
Wholemeal Rolls (page 212)

SAVOURY VEGETABLE CURRY

For this I use almost any vegetables in season, adding them at different points so that none is overcooked, but this is the basic recipe. Pulses and lentils, including *dhall*, may be cooked separately and added.

Imperial (Metric)
2 onions, each cut into 8 wedges
1-2 cloves garlic, crushed
2-3 tablespoonsful turmeric
3-4 tablespoonsful vegetable oil
1 small chilli pepper, dried or fresh, chopped
Pinch each of garam masala, cumin, fennel,
  coriander and mustard seeds
Freshly grated root ginger to taste
Sea salt and freshly ground black pepper

American
2 onions, each cut into 8 wedges
1-2 cloves garlic, crushed
2-3 tablespoonsful turmeric
4 tablespoonsful vegetable oil
1 small chilli pepper, dried or fresh, chopped
Pinch each of garam masala, cumin, fennel,
  coriander and mustard seeds
Freshly grated root ginger to taste
Sea salt and freshly ground black pepper

1. Heat the oil, gently brown the onions and garlic and the chilli.

2. Stir in the spices, pepper and salt.

3. Cook for 1 minute, then add any combination of seasonal vegetables—carrot sticks, celery slices, shredded cabbage, pepper rings and roughly diced potato, for example.

3. Brown the ingredients well, then add ½ pint (¼ litre) vegetable stock or water and *Marmite, Tastex, Vecon* or tomato paste (a strong solution). Cover the pan and simmer gently for 10 minutes.

4 Gradually add the remaining ingredients, stirring the sauce and covering the pot between each addition. Cook for about 45 minutes at the most, and check the flavour before removing from the heat. (Apple slices brushed with lemon juice and large Californian or Australian raisins are zesty sambals for this dish.)

SPINACH TAGLIATELLE IN TOMATO SAUCE

Imperial (Metric)
½ lb (¼ kilo) spinach-flavoured or wholemeal
   tagliatelle
1 lb (½ kilo) spinach
1 large onion, diced
2 cloves garlic, crushed
4 tablespoonsful vegetable oil
2 oz (50g) wholemeal flour
1 medium-sized tin tomatoes
1 teaspoonful tomato paste
1 teaspoonful *Vecon*, dissolved in a little water
Pinch of basil
½ pint (¼ litre) water
4 tablespoonsful skimmed milk powder
2 oz (50g) sunflower seeds
Grated Cheddar or Parmesan cheese to garnish

American
1½ cupsful (raw) spinach-flavoured or
   wholemeal tagliatelle
1 lb spinach
1 large onion, diced
2 cloves garlic, crushed
5 tablespoonsful vegetable oil
½ cupful wholemeal flour
1 medium-sized tin tomatoes
1 teaspoonful tomato paste
1 teaspoonful *Vecon*, dissolved in a little water
Pinch of basil
1¼ cupsful water
5 tablespoonsful skimmed milk powder
½ cupful sunflower seeds
Grated Cheddar or Parmesan cheese to garnish

1. Wash, drain and shred the spinach finely.

2. Place 1 tablespoonful of the oil in a heavy frying pan and *sauté* the onion and garlic until golden.

3. Add the spinach and *Vecon* and stir-fry over a medium heat until tender.

4. Meanwhile, cook the noodles.

5. Combine the noodles and spinach and set the mixture aside in a warm place.

6. Make a roux using the remaining oil and the flour. Cook for 1 minute then add the tomatoes and basil, whisking briskly.

7. As the sauce thickens, add the water and milk powder (mixed) and continue cooking.

8. Add the tomato paste and a little freshly ground black pepper.

9. Arrange a little of the sauce and the noodles in a shallow greased ovenproof dish. Pour the remaining sauce over the top and sprinkle with the seeds and grated cheese.

10. Bake at 350°F/180°C (Gas Mark 4) until bubbly and brown on top.

VEGETABLE RISOTTO

This risotto is based on the recipe for Mixed Vegetables and Tomatoes (page 139).

After the onion and garlic have been *sautéed*, add about 3 oz (75g) of brown rice, coating it with the oil. Then add those vegetables which need most cooking, together with the tomato paste, herbs and seasonings. Pour 1 pint (½ litre) water, mixed with a little *Marmite* or *Vecon* if desired, into the pan and stir gently. Cover and cook for about 20 minutes, stirring occasionally, and adding vegetables according to the amount of cooking they require.

Noodles may be used instead of rice, but remember to adjust the cooking time accordingly.

Note: A very useful lunchtime dish is made by grating or shredding and stir-frying a variety of vegetables, such as: onions and garlic, Chinese leaves, celery, fennel, peppers, carrots. Add a little vegetable stock and a quantity of ready-cooked rice to the pan. Cover and simmer over a low heat for a few minutes.

WINTER STEW

Imperial (Metric)	American
1 carrot, cut into rings	1 carrot, cut into rings
1 potato, cut into sticks	1 potato, cut into sticks
1 parsnip, diced	1 parsnip, diced
1 turnip, diced	1 turnip, diced
1 swede, diced	1 swede, diced
1 large onion, sliced	1 large onion, sliced
1 clove garlic, crushed	1 clove garlic, crushed
1 teaspoonful tomato paste or *Vecon*	1 teaspoonful tomato paste or *Vecon*
Pinch of fresh thyme	Pinch of fresh thyme
Grated cheese to garnish	Grated cheese to garnish

1. Cook the vegetables in very little water until tender but still crisp. Nearly all of the water should be absorbed.

2. Add the thyme and tomato paste or *Vecon*. Mix well and serve topped with plenty of grated cheese.

WINTER VEGETABLE SOUFFLÉ

Imperial (Metric)	American
1 lb (½ kilo) calabrese or	1 lb calabrese or
1 lb (½ kilo) Brussels sprouts	1 lb Brussels sprouts
1 large onion, diced	1 large onion, diced
4 oz (100g) mushrooms, sliced (optional)	2 cupsful mushrooms, sliced (optional)
1 carrot or potato, diced	1 carrot or potato, diced
2 oz (50g) Parmesan cheese, grated	½ cupful Parmesan cheese, grated
1 tablespoonful sesame seeds	1 tablespoonful sesame seeds
3 oz (75g) butter	⅓ cupful butter
3 oz (75g) wholemeal flour	¾ cupful wholemeal flour
1 pint (½ litre) milk or	2½ cupsful milk or
½ pint (¼ litre) milk and	1¼ cupsful milk and
¼ pint (150ml) each cream and vegetable stock	¾ cupful each cream and vegetable stock
3 eggs, separated	3 eggs, separated
Pinch of nutmeg, freshly grated	Pinch of nutmeg, freshly grated
Sea salt and freshly ground black pepper	Sea salt and freshly ground black pepper

1. Steam the green vegetables, carrots and potatoes until just cooked but still very crisp. Set them aside to drain, reserving the water for stock.

2. *Sauté* the mushrooms and onion in half of the butter until the onion is just transparent. Add the remaining butter, the flour and cheese and cook over a low heat for 1 minute.

3. Remove the pan from the heat and gradually add the liquid, whisking constantly. Return to the heat and stir the sauce until it thickens. Season and allow to cool slightly before beating in the egg yolks one by one.

4. Stiffly beat the egg whites.

5. Stir the vegetables into the sauce and fold in the egg whites very carefully.

6. Pour the mixture into a deep ovenproof buttered dish, leaving plenty of room for the *soufflé* to rise.

7. Sprinkle with sesame seeds and bake at 350°F/180°C (Gas Mark 4) for 50-60 minutes.

Sweet Dishes

APRICOT ALMOND DELIGHT

Imperial (Metric)
½ lb (¼ kilo) dried apricots
½ lb (¼ kilo) stoned dates
4 oz (100g) raisins
½ lb (¼ kilo) ground almonds or ground
  sunflower seeds
Juice and rind of 1 lemon
Orange juice to bind
Ground almonds, wheat germ or coconut

American
1½ cupsful dried apricots
1 cupful stoned dates
⅔ cupful raisins
1½ cupsful ground almonds or ground
  sunflower seeds
Juice and rind of 1 lemon
Orange juice to bind
Ground almonds, wheat germ or coconut

1. Mince the fruit and blend with as little juice as possible.

2. Mix in the ground almonds or seeds and roll teaspoonsful of the mixture in the almonds,
   wheat germ or coconut. (If the mixture seems too soft, add more almonds.) Chill to firm.

AUSTRALIAN CHRISTMAS CAKE

Imperial (Metric)
½ lb (¼ kilo) whole Brazil nuts
½ lb (¼ kilo) walnut halves
½ lb (¼ kilo) stoned dates
4 oz (100g) candied peel, chopped
6 oz (200g) maraschino cherries
3 oz (75g) raisins
4 oz (100g) wholemeal flour
½ teaspoonful baking powder
½ teaspoonful sea salt
½ lb (¼ kilo) raw cane sugar
3 eggs
1 teaspoonful pure vanilla essence

American
2 cupsful whole Brazil nuts
2 cupsful walnut halves
1 cupful stoned dates
1 cupful candied peel, chopped
1 cupful maraschino cherries
½ cupful raisins
1 cupful wholemeal flour
½ teaspoonful baking powder
½ teaspoonful sea salt
1 cupful raw cane sugar
3 eggs
1 teaspoonful pure vanilla essence

1.   Grease and line an 8×5 in. loaf tin.

2.   Mix the fruit and nuts (left whole) in a large bowl.

3.   Add the sugar to the sifted dry ingredients and mix this with the fruit and nuts.

4.   Add the beaten eggs and vanilla essence. Flatten the mixture in the tin, cover with foil and bake for 2½ hours at 250°F/130°C (Gas Mark ½). Remove the foil for the last half hour of baking and leave the cake in the tin for 10 minutes before turning it out. Store in the refrigerator when cold, and serve cut into thin slices.

BAKED APPLES

Imperial (Metric)
1-2 large Bramley apples per person

American
1-2 large Bramley apples per person

For each apple use:

1 tablespoonful dried raisins, sultanas or dates
4-5 almonds (whole)
½ teaspoonful mixed spice
½ teaspoonful molasses sugar (optional)
½ teaspoonful coconut (optional)
Knob of butter

1 tablespoonful dried raisins, sultanas or dates
4-5 almonds (whole)
½ teaspoonful mixed spice
½ teaspoonful molasses sugar (optional)
½ teaspoonful coconut (optional)
Knob of butter

1.   Core each apple, leaving a large central cylinder for the stuffing.

2.   Using a sharp, pointed knife, make shallow cuts in the peel in a spiral shape—this allows the apple to expand during cooking and makes the finished dish rather pretty.

3.   Mix the fruit, sugar and spices together with the coconut.

4.   Arrange the almonds lengthwise in the base of the central cylinder in the apple, wedging them in so that they form a firm 'floor' for the stuffing.

5. Stuff the apples tightly with the fruit mixture and arrange them, well spaced, in a lightly greased ovenproof dish. Top each one with a knob of butter and sprinkle with grated nutmeg or cinnamon.

6. Bake for 20-30 minutes at 350°F/180°C (Gas Mark 4), but be careful that the apples cook fairly gently.

Alternative Stuffing:

For each apple use:

1 tablespoonful ground almonds	1 tablespoonful ground almonds
1 dessertspoonful desiccated coconut	1 tablespoonful desiccated coconut
1 dessertspoonful wheat germ	1 tablespoonful wheat germ
1 teaspoonful molasses sugar	1 teaspoonful molasses sugar
¼ teaspoonful cinnamon	¼ teaspoonful cinnamon
Egg yolk to bind	Egg yolk to bind

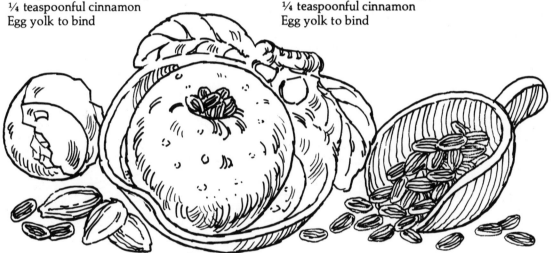

BRANDIED APRICOTS

Imperial (Metric)
1 lb (½ kilo) dried whole apricots, well washed
3 oz (75g) raw cane sugar
¼ pint (150ml) water
Brandy to cover

American
3 cupsful dried whole apricots, well washed
¼ cupful raw cane sugar
¾ cupful water
Brandy to cover

1. Boil the sugar and water together to make a syrup.

2. Pile the fruit into a clean screw-topped glass jar with a well fitting lid.

3. Pour the syrup into the jar, then completely cover the fruit with brandy.

4. Cover the jar with clingfilm, then screw on the lid and cover with more clingfilm. Gently invert the jar to distribute the brandy.

5. Leave in a cool, dark place for at least 1 month, but the longer the better. Top up with brandy occasionally if necessary. Serve the apricots in the liquor with some cream. Alternatively, serve the liquor in glasses beside the apricots.

BRANDY BUTTER

Imperial (Metric)
4 oz (100g) unsalted butter, soft
½ lb (¼ kilo) raw cane sugar, finely ground in
  a blender
4 tablespoonsful brandy

American
½ cupful unsalted butter, soft
1⅓ cupsful raw cane sugar, finely ground in
  in a blender
5 tablespoonsful brandy

1. Cream the butter with an electric beater, whisk or wooden spoon.

2. Gradually add the sugar, beating until light and fluffy, then slowly mix in the brandy. Adjust the flavour to suit your taste.

3. Pile the butter onto a serving dish, making decorative peaks with a fork, and leave to harden in the refrigerator.

4. Cover with clingfilm to store. The butter should keep for a week or so. Garnish with toasted flaked almonds and slivers of angelica and other *glacé* fruit. Serve with Christmas pudding.

CAKE: BASIC RECIPE

Imperial (Metric)
½ lb (¼ kilo) wholemeal flour
3 teaspoonsful baking powder
4 oz (100g) butter, melted or
3 tablespoonsful vegetable oil
¼ pint (150ml) milk or water
2 eggs
2 tablespoonsful unset honey

American
2 cupsful wholemeal flour
3 teaspoonsful baking powder
½ cupful butter, melted or
4 tablespoonsful vegetable oil
¾ cupful milk or water
2 eggs
2½ tablespoonsful unset honey

1. Sift the flour and baking powder into the mixing bowl.

2. Beat the eggs and mix in the milk and honey. Add this mixture to the dry ingredients, and beat well with a wooden spoon.

3. Add the butter or oil and beat again until the colour of the mixture lightens a little.

4. Bake for 40 minutes in a greased and lined tin at 350°F/180°C (Gas Mark 4).

CANTALOUPE AND PASSION FRUIT SALAD

For each person arrange a wedge of cantaloupe melon with the flesh of a passion fruit scooped over it. Home-made vanilla ice cream (page 110) goes perfectly with this combination.

CITRUS FRUIT SALAD

Peel, thinly slice across the segments and combine 1 orange, 1 grapefruit, 2 mandarins or satsumas, 3-4 clementines and 1-2 kumquats. Toss the fruit in the juice and grated rind of 1 lemon or lime.

COTTAGE CHEESE AND APRICOT FOOL

Imperial (Metric)
½ lb (¼ kilo) sun-dried apricots, soaked overnight
½ lb (¼ kilo) cottage cheese, sieved
2 tablespoonsful soured cream (optional)
½ teaspoonful mixed spice
Honey to taste

American
1½ cupsful sun-dried apricots, soaked overnight
1 cupful cottage cheese, sieved
2½ tablespoonsful soured cream (optional)
½ teaspoonful mixed spice
Honey to taste

1. Poach the apricots in a little water and *purée* them in a blender with the other ingredients.

Variations
Similar dishes may be prepared using thick *purées* of the following fruits:

Stewed apples and stem ginger in syrup;

Stewed damsons flavoured with cinnamon;

Fresh raspberries with a little Kirsch;

Fresh strawberries with a little brandy.

COTTAGE CHEESE AND HAZELNUTS

Imperial (Metric)
½ lb (¼ kilo) cottage cheese, sieved
2 tablespoonful double or single cream
4 oz (100g) toasted hazelnuts, ground or
   finely chopped
4 oz (100g) toasted hazelnuts, whole
2 tablespoonful *Tia Maria*

American
1 cupful cottage cheese, sieved
2½ tablespoonful double or single cream
¾ cupful toasted hazelnuts, ground or finely
   chopped
1 cupful toasted hazelnuts, whole
2½ tablespoonful *Tia Maria*

1. Mix all the ingredients together well except for the whole hazelnuts.

2. Set the mixture aside in a cool place for an hour or so and then decorate with the whole nuts.

COTTAGE CHEESE AND WALNUTS

Imperial (Metric)
½ lb (¼ kilo) cottage cheese, sieved
4 oz (100g) walnuts, chopped
2 tablespoonful maraschino cherries with
   just a little of their syrup
Lemon juice to taste

American
1 cupful cottage cheese, sieved
1 cupful walnuts, chopped
2½ tablespoonful maraschino cherries with
   just a little of their syrup
Lemon juice to taste

1. Gently fold the nuts and cherries into the cheese, adding lemon juice if the flavour is too sweet.

2. Decorate with walnut halves.

DATE AND CASHEW ROUNDS

Imperial (Metric)
½ lb (¼ kilo) dates, stoned and finely chopped
4-6 oz (100-200g) cashew nuts, ground
Juice of 1-2 oranges
Bran

American
1 cupful dates, stoned and finely chopped
1-1½ cupsful cashew nuts, ground
Juice of 1-2 oranges
Bran

1. In the blender, on a slow speed, *purée* the dates with the orange juice, using as little juice as possible—a rough *purée* is sufficient.

2. Add the cashews until the mixture is of rolling consistency.

3. Roll teaspoonful of the mixture in the bran, then flatten each one.

4. Place on wire racks or plates to dry out a little more. (The bran will absorb some of the moisture.)

DRIED FRUIT SALADS

To reconstitute dried fruit, simply soak it in fresh water for up to 12 hours. The fruit will plump up quickest in water, but on special occasions use other fruit juice, wine, brandy or rum. The stronger and sweeter the liquid, the longer the time required to reconstitute the fruit.

The following combinations of dried fruit are highly concentrated and should only be served occasionally:

Platter of figs, prunes, apricots and peaches;

De-seeded prunes, stuffed with sunflower seeds or cottage cheese, flavoured with lemon rind;

Bowls of sultanas, raisins, currants, almonds, walnuts, hazelnuts or seeds.

GRAPEFRUIT DESSERT

For each person take half a grapefruit and loosen the flesh around the edge of the peel. Sprinkle with sherry and raw cane sugar and set aside for an hour or so. Garnish with a sprig of fresh mint. Alternatively, sprinkle raw cane sugar over the grapefruit and flash it under the grill until the sugar melts and begins to bubble.

LEMON SORBET

Imperial (Metric)
¼ pint (150ml) fresh lemon juice
2 oz (50g) raw cane sugar
½ pint (¼ litre) water

American
¾ cupful fresh lemon juice
⅓ cupful raw cane sugar
1¼ cupful water

1. Boil the sugar and water together for 5 minutes to make a syrup.

2. Mix in the juice and pour into an ice cream tray and freeze to a soft ice consistency.

3. Spoon the mixture into small stemmed glasses and garnish with a slice of fresh lemon.

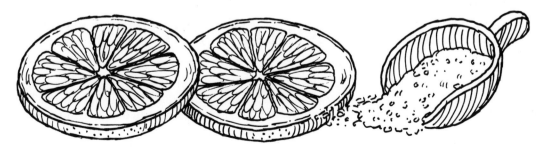

LIGHT CHRISTMAS PUDDING

Imperial (Metric)	American
¾ lb (350g) wholemeal breadcrumbs	6 cupsful wholemeal breadcrumbs
2 tablespoonful sunflower seed oil	2½ tablespoonsful sunflower seed oil
6 oz (200g) raisins	1 cupful raisins
½ lb (¼ kilo) currants	1¼ cupsful currants
4 oz (100g) sultanas	¾ cupful sultanas
2 oz (50g) candied peel	½ cupful candied peel
1 small apple, grated	1 small apple, grated
1 small carrot, grated	1 small carrot, grated
2 oz (50g) almonds, chopped	½ cupful almonds, chopped
2 large eggs, beaten	2 large eggs, beaten
½ teaspoonful freshly grated nutmeg	½ teaspoonful freshly grated nutmeg
1 teaspoonful mixed spice	1 teaspoonful mixed spice
1 small bottle *Guinness*	1 small bottle *Guinness*
Grated rind of 1 orange and 1 lemon	Grated rind of 1 orange and 1 lemon

1. Combine all the ingredients except for the *Guinness* and mix well.

2. Gradually add the stout to make a moist but firm mixture and combine thoroughly. (1-2 tablespoonsful of brandy may replace some of the stout.)

3. Proceed as in the recipe for Rich Christmas Pudding (page 206). This pudding can be made about 2 weeks in advance, steam it for 4 hours then and 3 hours on the day of eating.

LYCHEES AND MELON FRUIT SALAD

Combine the basic fruit salad (page 108) with ½ lb (¼ kilo) lychees, peeled, stoned and halved, ½ large honeydew or ogen melon, scooped out in balls and 1 kiwi fruit, diced. Toss the fruit in a syrup made from 1 tablespoonful of honey, 1 tablespoonful of water and the juice of 1 lemon.

MIXED FRUIT CANDY

Imperial (Metric)
1 lb (½ kilo) stoned dates, chopped
1 lb (½ kilo) dried apricots, chopped
3-4 oz (75-100g) dried figs, chopped
3-4 oz (75-100g) almonds
3 oz (75g) toasted sesame seeds
2 teaspoonsful honey
2 oz (50g) coconut

American
2 cupsful stoned dates, chopped
2 cupsful dried apricots, chopped
½-¾ cupful dried figs, chopped
½-¾ cupful almonds
½ cupful toasted sesame seeds
2 teaspoonsful honey
⅔ cupful coconut

1. Mix the fruit, except the coconut, nuts and seeds together with the honey.

2. Roll the mixture into a long sausage shape and cover with the coconut. Chill in the refrigerator and serve sliced.

RASPBERRY JELLY

Use frozen raspberries for this recipe. Defrost the fruit thoroughly and push it through a fine sieve to remove the seeds. Sweeten the *purée* with very little raw cane sugar, leaving the taste quite sharp. Heat a little of the *purée* and sprinkle over 2 teaspoonsful of agar-agar for each pint of fluid. Whisk the mixture, adding the remaining *purée* gradually so that the agar-agar dissolves smoothly. Pour into small glasses, leave to set, then top with one undefrosted raspberry. This will gradually defrost as the jelly waits to be served and so remain firm.

RICH CHRISTMAS PUDDING

Imperial (Metric)	American
1 medium-sized block creamed coconut (*Sharwoods*), grated	1 medium-sized block creamed coconut (*Sharwoods*), grated
5 oz (150g) butter or	⅔ cupful butter or
4 tablespoonsful sunflower seed oil	5 tablespoonsful sunflower seed oil
10 oz (300g) wholemeal breadcrumbs	5 cupsful wholemeal breadcrumbs
5 oz (150g) wholemeal flour	1¼ cupsful wholemeal flour
½ lb (¼ kilo) sun-dried raisins	1¼ cupsful sun-dried raisins
10 oz (300g) sun-dried sultanas	1½ cupsful sun-dried sultanas
5 oz (150g) apple, freshly grated	1 cupful apple, freshly grated
4 large eggs	4 large eggs
4 oz (100g) candied peel, chopped small	1 cupful candied peel, chopped small
2 oz (50g) almonds, chopped	½ cupful almonds, chopped
½ teaspoonful nutmeg, freshly grated	½ teaspoonful nutmeg, freshly grated
1 teaspoonful mixed spice	1 teaspoonful mixed spice
3 oz (75g) Barbados sugar	½ cupful dark brown sugar
1 sherry glassful rum or brandy	1 sherry glassful rum or brandy
½ sherry glassful sherry	½ sherry glassful sherry
1 sherry glassful stout (*Guinness*)	1 sherry glassful stout (*Guinness*)
Freshly grated rind and juice of ½-1 lemon	Freshly grated rind and juice of ½-1 lemon

1. Soak the fruit in the spirit and sherry.

2. Place the flour in a large mixing bowl and rub in the butter or oil.

3. Add the grated coconut cream, breadcrumbs, sugar, almonds, lemon rind, nutmeg, spice and apple.

4. Add the fruit mixture. Beat the eggs and add them to the stout and lemon juice. Stir well, then add this to the flour and fruit mixture, gradually stirring it in so that the ingredients are thoroughly combined.

5. Put the mixture into greased basins leaving about 1 in. below the rim. Place circles of greased brown paper over the puddings.

6. Secure lids or make lids by measuring a square of aluminium foil large enough to make a pleat across the centre top of the bowl. (Line the foil with butter paper to prevent it contaminating the food.)

7. Press the foil down around the sides and tie firmly with string. Boilable, non-polluting plastic bowls with lids are very efficient for making puddings.

8. Steam the puddings for 6-8 hours. Allow them to cool then store in a cool dry place, and re-steam for 3-4 hours on the day of use. (The longer the cooking time, the darker the pudding. This pudding will keep well for a year, so make enough for two years at a time. It may be preferable to use four small bowls, about 1-1½ pints (½-¾ litre) in size, rather than one or two larger bowls. One quarter of the mixture will serve six people.)

9. When ready to serve, gently heat about 2 tablespoonful of brandy over a low flame. Loosen the pudding by sliding a knife around its edge, then turn it out onto a large flat dish. Pour the brandy over the top and set light to it. Serve immediately.

   (Left-over pudding often seems unappetizing, but it is delicious if sliced fairly thinly, fried for a few minutes each side in butter, arranged on a platter and sprinkled with raw cane sugar. Serve with brandy butter (page 200), double cream flavoured with port, or home-made ice cream (page 110).

RUSSIAN CREAM NOELA

Imperial (Metric)	American
6 oz (200g) curd cheese or cream cheese	¾ cupful curd cheese or cream cheese
1 teaspoonful lemon juice	1 teaspoonful lemon juice
2 oz (50g) raw cane sugar	¼ cupful raw cane sugar
2 oz (50g) raisins	⅔ cupful raisins
2 oz (50g) sultanas	⅔ cupful sultanas
2 oz (50g) nuts, grated	⅓ cupful nuts, grated
1-2 oz (25-50g) whole nuts (optional)	¼-½ cupful whole nuts (optional)
½ pint (¼ litre) milk	1¼ cupsful milk
Grated rind of ½ lemon	Grated rind of ½ lemon

1. Beat the cheese and milk to a thick cream.

2. Fold in the remaining ingredients and mix well.

3. Serve decorated with some nuts and dried fruit in a stoneware bowl.

SESAME CANDY

Imperial (Metric)	American
1 cupful tahini	1¼ cupful tahini
½ cupful honey	⅔ cupful honey
2 tablespoonsful coconut	2½ tablespoonsful coconut
2-3 oz (50-75g) nuts, chopped	½-¾ cupful nuts, chopped
4 tablespoonsful carob powder	5 tablespoonsful carob powder
3 tablespoonsful powdered milk	4 tablespoonsful powdered milk
Toasted sesame seeds	Toasted sesame seeds

1. Combine all the ingredients except for the seeds thoroughly.

2. Roll balls of the mixture in the toasted sesame seeds and set aside to firm up.

SPICE CAKE

Imperial (Metric)	American
Ingredients for the basic cake recipe (page 200)	Ingredients for the basic cake recipe (page 200)
2 teaspoonsful mixed spice or garam masala	2 teaspoonsful mixed spice or garam masala
1 teaspoonful cinnamon or ginger	1 teaspoonful cinnamon or ginger
1 tablespoonful vegetable oil	1 tablespoonful vegetable oil
1 tablespoonful raw cane sugar	1 tablespoonful raw cane sugar
1 teaspoonful mixed spice	1 teaspoonful mixed spice

1. Add the two teaspoonsful of mixed spice or garam masala with the cinnamon or ginger to the basic dry ingredients.

2. Proceed as for the basic cake recipe and when the cake is cooked but still warm, brush the top with vegetable oil and sprinkle the sugar and mixed spice over the top.

WHITE SAUCE

This traditional accompaniment to Christmas pudding is often scorned, but its blandness and satiny smoothness make it a perfect foil for the fruitiness of the pudding for those who find cream too rich.

Imperial (Metric)	American
2 oz (50g) 81 per cent wholemeal flour	½ cupful 81 per cent wholemeal flour
2 oz (50g) butter	¼ cupful butter
1 pint (½ litre) milk, half of it warmed	2½ cupsful milk, half of it warmed
1 oz (25g) raw cane sugar*	2½ tablespoonsful raw cane sugar*
Few drops of pure vanilla essence	Few drops of pure vanilla essence
Sherry or brandy to taste (optional)	Sherry or brandy to taste (optional)

1. Melt the butter over a low heat and add the flour, stirring and cooking for 1 minute.

2. Remove the pan from the heat and add the cold milk, whisking well and returning to the heat.

3. Gradually whisk in the warmed milk, sugar and vanilla essence to form a light satiny texture.

4. Remove the pan from the heat when the sauce coats the whisk. Stir in the alcohol.

If this is to be the only accompaniment, it may be enriched by replacing a few tablespoonsful of the milk with cream. (Never boil this sauce.) If it is to be kept warm, cover the surface with very lightly buttered paper as well as a lid and this will prevent a skin forming.

*The use of unrefined sugar may alter the flavour and colour of this sauce which is usually made with white sugar.

WINE FRUIT MINCE

Any combination of dried fruits, chopped finely or minced;
1 medium-sized tin crushed pineapple;
Fresh lemon or orange rind;
Barbados sugar (dark brown sugar) to taste;
Mixed spice or garam masala to taste;
Dry sherry or red table wine.

1. Combine the dry ingredients and pineapple and place the mixture in a large screw-top jar with a tight-fitting lid.

2. Cover with the wine or sherry, screw the lid on tightly and seal with clingfilm. This mince will keep for months or even years. It is delicious if blended smooth in a liquidizer, heated gently with a little extra liquid and then served with home-made ice cream (page 110).

Breads and Biscuits

BREAD: BASIC RECIPE

Imperial (Metric)
2 lb (1 kilo) wholemeal flour
2 teaspoonsful kelp powder or sea salt
4 teaspoonsful dried bakers' yeast or
1½ oz (40g) fresh yeast
1 dessertspoonful molasses (not necessary if
  using fresh yeast)
1 pint (½ litre) tepid water

American
8 cupsful wholemeal flour
2 teaspoonsful kelp powder or sea salt
4 teaspoonsful dried bakers' yeast or
1½ tabelspoonsful fresh yeast
1 tablespoonful molasses (not necessary if
  using fresh yeast)
2½ cupsful tepid water

1. Add the molasses to the water, stir to dissolve and sprinkle the yeast over the top. Leave in a warm place for a few minutes.

2. Meanwhile, measure the flour and salt or kelp into a large bowl, make a well in the centre and pour in the yeast mixture.

3. Mix thoroughly with a wooden spoon, then turn out onto a floured board and knead until the dough is firm but not sticky and can be shaped into two loaves.

4. Place the loaves in two oiled double-based loaf tins and put them in two plastic bags. Leave in a warm place until the dough has risen nearly to the top of the tins. (If bubbles form on the top the dough has over-proved, in which case knock it down and let it rise once more.)

5. Bake the loaves at 400°F/200°C (Gas Mark 6) for 30 minutes. If properly cooked, the loaves will have a hollow ring when tapped with the fingers.

6. Leave the loaves in the tins for a few minutes, then turn out and wrap in clean cloths. Leave for 24 hours before storing in a bread crock or plastic bags.

Variations

i. 2-3 tablespoonsful sesame, sunflower or poppy seeds; oatmeal, wheat germ or wheat bran.

ii. 2 teaspoonsful herbs.

iii. 1 onion, chopped

iv. 2-4 oz (50-100g) cheese, grated.

v. 2 oz (50g) nuts, chopped

Any of these variations may be included in the basic recipe. If liked, the loaves may also be glazed with the yolk of an egg and sprinkled with seeds or nuts while still hot.

BREAD ROLLS

Follow the basic bread recipe (page 211). This quantity of dough will make two dozen rolls.

1. Brush two patty tins with vegetable oil.

2. Divide the dough into two and roll it into log shapes with the hands.

3. Divide each 'log' into 12 pieces and knead each one into shape to fit the tins.

4. Bake for 12-15 minutes at 375°F/190°C (Gas Mark 5) and leave to cool for a few minutes before removing the rolls from the tins. Serve hot or cold.

These little rolls are a good idea when you are in a hurry as they can be eaten almost immediately after baking. They are particularly good with Ratatouille (page 98).

Variations

Swirl: Roll each piece of dough into a pencil shape and curl it up.

Trefoil: Divide each piece of dough into three and roll into balls, placing them together in the tin.

Plait: Roll each piece of dough into a thin pencil shape, fold each one in half and twist the ends over each other. Roll up the plait to fit the tin.

Bun: Roll each piece of dough on a floured board under the cupped hand.

CHEESE BALLS

Imperial (Metric)	*American*
1 oz (25g) Parmesan cheese, grated	¼ cupful Parmesan cheese, grated
3 oz (75g) Cheddar cheese, grated	1 cupful Cheddar cheese, grated
3 oz (75g) butter	⅓ cupful butter
6 oz (200g) wholemeal flour	1½ cupsful wholemeal flour
½ teaspoonful dry mustard	½ teaspoonful dry mustard
Pinch each of cayenne pepper and sea salt	Pinch each of cayenne pepper and sea salt
Poppy seeds, toasted sesame seeds or coconut	Poppy seeds, toasted sesame seeds or coconut

1. Rub the butter and the cheeses into the dry ingredients to make a firm dough.

2. Shape the dough into little balls about ¾ in. in diameter and roll them in poppy seeds, toasted sesame seeds or coconut.

3. Bake, well separated, on greased trays at 350°F/180°C (Gas Mark 4) for 12-15 minutes.

GINGERBREAD MEN

Imperial (Metric)
10 oz (300g) wholemeal flour
1 teaspoonful baking powder
2 teaspoonsful ground ginger
½ teaspoonful bicarbonate of soda
3 oz (75g) butter
3 oz (75g) Barbados sugar
2 tablespoonsful golden syrup
Currants and nuts to decorate

American
2½ cupsful wholemeal flour
1 teaspoonful baking powder
2 teaspoonsful ground ginger
½ teaspoonful baking soda
⅓ cupful butter
⅓ cupful dark brown sugar
2½ tablespoonsful golden syrup
Currants and nuts to decorate

1. Sift together the dry ingredients.

2. Gently melt together the butter, sugar and syrup. Allow the mixture to cool slightly, then pour it into the dry ingredients, mixing well with a wooden spoon.

3. Set aside to firm up then knead the dough lightly.

4. Roll the dough out on a well floured board to about ¼ in. thickness, cut out the gingerbread men and decorate them.

5. Arrange the figures, well spaced, on oiled trays and bake at 350°F/180°C (Gas Mark 4) for 10 minutes only.

6. Allow the gingerbread men to cool a little before removing them from the trays with a knife and placing them on wire racks to cool completely. (Gingerbread cats and dogs with the trimmings are very popular too.)

HONEY AND OAT BISCUITS

Imperial (Metric)
5 heaped tablespoonsful rolled oats
4 tablespoonsful vegetable oil
1 tablespoonful honey
2 tablespoonsful raisins or sultanas
2 tablespoonsful cashews or peanuts
1 teaspoonful each ginger and cinnamon or
   mixed spice

American
6 heaped tablespoonsful rolled oats
5 tablespoonsful vegetable oil
1 tablespoonful honey
2½ tablespoonsful raisins or sultanas
2½ tablespoonsful cashews or peanuts
1 teaspoonful each ginger and cinnamon or
   mixed spice

1. Heat together the oil and honey, stirring to combine the two.

2. Add the remaining ingredients and mix well.

3. Spoon the mixture into a shallow oiled baking tin, levelling the surface with the back of the spoon.

4. Bake for 20 minutes at 325°F/170°C (Gas Mark 3).

5. Allow the mixture to cool in the tin before cutting it into squares. Store the biscuits in an air-tight container.

HONEY BUTTER BISCUITS

Imperial (Metric)
4 tablespoonsful butter
2 tablespoonsful honey
6 oz (200g) rolled oats
2 oz (50g) wholemeal flour
1 egg, beaten
Few drops of pure vanilla essence

American
5 tablespoonsful butter
2½ tablespoonsful honey
1½ cupsful rolled oats
½ cupful wholemeal flour
1 egg, beaten
Few drops of pure vanilla essence

1. Melt the butter and honey together, add the oats, flour and essence and mix in the egg.

2. Place spoonsful of the mixture in oiled patty tins or on an oiled baking tray and bake for 12 minutes at 350°F/180°C (Gas Mark 4).

HOT BREADS

Use long, French stick-shaped loaves, sliced very thick, but not cut all the way through. Spread one side of each slice thickly with one of the following mixtures:

Butter, sea salt and freshly ground black pepper; with either chopped parsley, chopped spring onions, crushed cloves of garlic, or herbs.

Wrap the loaf in tin foil and bake for 10 minutes at 375°F/190°C (Gas Mark 5). Serve the broken loaf in baskets with salad, cheese, etc.

OAT AND FRUIT BISCUITS

Imperial (Metric)
3 oz (75g) raw cane sugar
4 oz (100g) butter
½ lb (¼kilo) rolled oats
1 egg
4 oz (100g) wholemeal flour
1-2 oz (25-50g) raisins
Few drops of pure vanilla essence
Pinch of freshly grated nutmeg
Milk to bind

American
⅓ cupful raw cane sugar
½ cupful butter
2 cupsful rolled oats
1 egg
1 cupful wholemeal flour
Approx. ½ cupful raisins
Few drops of pure vanilla essence
Pinch of freshly grated nutmeg
Milk to bind

1. Cream the butter and sugar.

2. Beat together the egg and vanilla essence.

3. Add the oats, nutmeg and raisins to the butter, then mix in the egg and essence.

4. Fold in the flour, adding a little milk if the mixture seems too dry.

5. Roll out the dough, cut biscuits out and place them on an oiled baking tray. Bake at 350°F/180°C (Gas Mark 4) for 30-35 minutes, then increase the heat to brown the biscuits.

OATMEAL MOLASSES BISCUITS

Imperial (Metric)
10 oz (300g) rolled oats
4 tablespoonful vegetable oil
½ teaspoonful cinnamon
¼ teaspoonful nutmeg
2 tablespoonsful molasses
2 tablespoonsful golden syrup
1 egg, lightly beaten

American
2½ cupsful rolled oats
5 tablespoonsful vegetable oil
½ teaspoonful cinnamon
¼ teaspoonful nutmeg
2½ tablespoonsful molasses
2½ tabelspoonsful golden syrup
1 egg, lightly beaten

1. Mix together the oil, molasses and golden syrup and heat gently.

2. Add the remaining ingredients, the egg last, and mix together with a wooden spoon.

3. Cook in a greased baking dish at 350°F/180°C (Gas Mark 4) for 20 minutes. (This will make a chewy consistency. Bake on a larger tray for crisper biscuits.)

4. Cut the mixture into fingers while still warm and leave to cool in the dish.

SESAME CRACKERS

Imperial (Metric)
10 oz (300g) wholemeal flour
½ teaspoonful sea salt
¼ teaspoonful cayenne pepper
¼ pint (150ml) vegetable oil
5 tablespoonsful iced water
3-4 oz (75-100g) sesame seeds, toasted

American
2½ cupsful wholemeal flour
½ teaspoonful sea salt
¼ teaspoonful cayenne pepper
¾ cupful vegetable oil
6 tablespoonsful iced water
½ cupful sesame seeds, toasted

1. Blend the dry ingredients with the oil and water. Stir in the seeds.

2. Roll the mixture out thinly, cut it into strips about 2 in. long and bake at 300°F/150°C (Gas Mark 2) for 15-20 minutes.

3. Crisp up in the oven after storage.

SUNSHINE BISCUITS

Imperial (Metric)
½ oz (15g) bran
2 oz (50g) wheat germ
2 oz (50g) sunflower seeds
3 oz (75g) sesame seeds
2 oz (50g) honey
2 oz (50g) melted butter or vegetable oil
½ teaspoonful cinnamon
1 large egg, beaten

American
½ cupful bran
½ cupful wheat germ
½ cupful sunflower seeds
½ cupful sesame seeds
¼ cupful honey
¼ cupful melted butter or vegetable oil
½ teaspoonful cinnamon
1 large egg, beaten

1. Combine all the ingredients.

2. For chewy biscuits, spread the mixture over a large oiled tray and bake at 300°F/150°C (Gas Mark 2) for 20 minutes and cut into fingers while still warm.

3. For crisp biscuits, bake teaspoonsful of the mixture on an oiled baking tray at 350°F/180°C (Gas Mark 4). Press sunflower seeds into the top to garnish before baking.

THE GRANT LOAF

The basic idea of this loaf is that 100 per cent wholemeal flour, because it is heavier than white flour, makes a dough that does not need to be kneaded. Doris Grant originated the loaf and I have modified it slightly.

Imperial (Metric)
1 dessertspoonful molasses or Barbados sugar
4 teaspoonsful dried yeast
1½ pints (¾ litre) warm water
2 lb (1 kilo) wholemeal flour
1 heaped teaspoonful kelp powder or sea salt

American
1 tablespoonful molasses or dark brown sugar
4 teaspoonsful dried yeast
3¾ cupsful warm water
8 cupsful wholemeal flour
1 heaped teaspoonful kelp powder or sea salt

1. Measure out 1 pint of the water. Dissolve the molasses or Barbados sugar in it and gradually sprinkle the yeast over the top.

2. Put the mixture in a warm place to fluff up the yeast—this takes about 10 minutes.

3. Meanwhile, mix together the flour and kelp or salt and set them aside to warm a little too.

4. Oil two 1 lb (½ kilo) loaf tins and warm them.

5. Combine the yeast and flour mixtures, and add up to ½ pint (¼ litre) water, mixing quickly and thoroughly but gently with a wooden spoon. Turn the dough into the loaf tins.

6. Cover the tins with a damp tea-towel and leave them in a warm place until the mixture rises by one third.

7. Bake the loaves at 400°F/200°C (Gas Mark 6) for 30-40 minutes. Leave to cool in the tin for about 15 minutes, then wrap each loaf in a clean tea-towel and leave to cool completely. The loaves may be stored in plastic clingfilm or greaseproof paper, covered with foil. This loaf keeps very well indeed and such an amount lasts our household of two adults and one child for a week.

THE SHEARS' SEVEN GRAIN LOAF

Imperial (Metric)

1 lb 10 oz (¾ kilo) wholewheat flour (stone-
    ground and compost-grown)
½ lb (¼ kilo) barley
4 oz (100g) oats
4 oz (100g) buckwheat
2 oz (50g) maize meal
2 oz (50g) soya
2 oz (50g) rye
2 oz (50g) mixed nuts, freshly ground
2 tablespoonful sunflower seed oil
2 pints (1 litre) warm water
4 teaspoonsful herb salt
4 teaspoonsful honey
2 oz (50g) fresh yeast or
1 oz (25g) dried yeast

American

4⅓ cupsful wholewheat flour (stone-ground
    and compost-grown)
1 cupful barley
1 cupful oats
1 cupful buckwheat
½ cupful maize meal
½ cupful soya
½ cupful rye
½ cupful mixed nuts, freshly ground
2½ tablespoonsful sunflower seed oil
5 cupsful warm water
4 teaspoonsful herb salt
4 teaspoonsful honey
2½ tablespoonsful fresh yeast or
1 tablespoonful dried yeast

1. Pour ½ pint (¼ litre) of warm water into a bowl with the crumbled yeast. Add the honey and set aside to froth up—this takes about 10 minutes.

2. Mix together all the dry ingredients and add the yeast mixture with the oil and the rest of the water. Combine thoroughly until all the flour is evenly wetted. The dough should then be slippery.

3. Knead until firm but not sticky. Divide the dough into three greased and floured 1 lb loaf tins. Put each tin into a heavy-duty plastic bag and leave the dough to rise by one third.

4. Bake for 1 hour at 350°F/180°C (Gas Mark 4).

Seasonal Vitalizing Diets

These seasonal diets may be used to rest the digestive system and to increase physical and mental vitality. They should not be used by those on medicines or in a doctor's care.

The following items should be eliminated from the diet: drugs, alcohol, soft drinks, cigarettes; coffee, tea, cocoa; salt, sugar, condiments; biscuits, cakes, white bread products; processed food. Read all labels on food.

Plenty of rest, quietness, fresh air and water should be taken when following a seasonal diet.

SPRING

1. *Fourteen days of:*
   Fruit for breakfast and dinner;
   Salad and protein for lunch.

2. *Followed by three days of:*
   Fruit for each meal.

3. *Finish with three days of:*
   Fruit for breakfast;
   Salad for lunch;
   Vegetables for dinner.

   Return to normal diet

SUMMER

1. *Three days of:*
   Fruit for each meal.

2. *Followed by three days of:*
   Water and diluted fruit juice.

3. *Followed by three days of:*
   Fruit for each meal.

Over the next week, gradually increase the variety of the diet by adding fruit and salads, then protein and vegetables and finally carbohydrates and fats.

AUTUMN

This season's special eliminative and vitalizing regime is simple:

One day each week of fruit for each meal;
and/or
One day each week of salad for each meal.

An Alternative Diet

Two days each week of:
Fruit or fruit juice for breakfast;
Salad for lunch;
Fruit for dinner.

Return to normal diet for the other days. Pursue this plan for about four weeks, or longer if you feel like it, but not less.

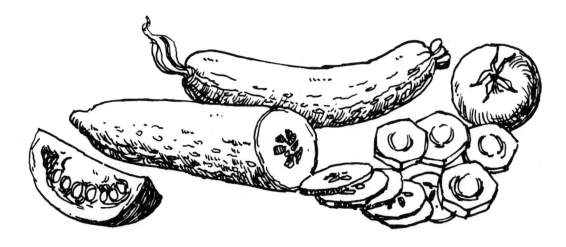

WINTER

Foods to be limited
Eggs—one weekly
Cheddar and other full-fat cheeses—once weekly
Wholemeal bread—one slice weekly
Potatoes—one weekly
Wholegrain rice—1-2 tablespoonsful weekly

Foods to be eaten regularly
Vegetables
Fruit Salads
Seeds
Seeds may be sprinkled over any meal or, alternatively,
have a piece of fruit after your salad.
Lactic or cottage cheese and yogurt—once daily
Drink plenty of water and apple juice

Note: Eat two meals daily, omitting whichever of the usual meals suits you, *but* work for an hour or so before eating *and* finish eating early in the evening—by about 7.30 p.m.

Fourteen Day Plan

Day	Fruit Meal	Salad or Vegetable Meal
1.	Stewed apple and ground almonds	Carrot and celery sticks
2.	Fresh fruit (one kind only)	Brussels sprouts and celery Salad with lactic cheese
3.	Stewed dried apricots with brown rice	Winter Break Salad (p. 174)
4.	Fresh Fruit Salad (p. 106) and almonds	Walnut Loaf (p. 146) with cheese, carrots and celery
5.	Fresh fruit and yogurt (p. 112)	1 slice of wholemeal bread with butter, *Marmite* and carrot or celery sticks
6.	Grapefruit and fresh or stewed apple	Cooked greens (e.g. Brussels sprouts, kale, sprout tops, cabbage, broccoli) and lactic or cottage cheese
7.	*Compote* of reconstituted dried fruit (e.g. apricots, sultanas, raisins, pears, peaches)	1 baked jacket potato, a little butter and *Marmite* with green salad (e.g. alfalfa sprouts, Brussels sprouts and watercress, if possible)
8.	Apple juice and ½ grapefruit	Carrot, Chinese leaves and lactic cheese
9.	Fresh fruit (one or two kinds)	Portion of a nut loaf with cooked parsnip or carrot and green vegetables
10.	Reconstituted dried fruit and yogurt (p. 112)	Beetroot and celery salad with onions or chives

11. Stewed, baked or fresh apple and ½ grapefruit	Pepper and mushroom salad with cottage or curd cheese
12. Banana and satsuma	Onion omelette and fresh bean sprouts (e.g. mung, alfalfa, aduki)
13. Dried peaches stewed in orange juice	Grated carrot and celery with yogurt (p. 112) or lactic cheese
14. Apple juice and grapefruit	Green vegetables with black pepper and butter

Twenty Dinner Party Menus

1.
Crudités and Cocktail Sauce (p. 124)
or
Stuffed Eggs (p. 80)

Ratatouille (p. 98) served with parsley, grated cheese and cashew nuts
Fresh Bread Rolls (p. 212) and butter
or
Hot Breads (p. 214)
Green salad

Russian Cream Noela (p. 207)
Orange and Date Salad (p. 59)

2.
Mushroom Soup (p. 126) with *croûtons*

Stuffed Aubergines (p. 99) with steamed vegetables
or
Stuffed Marrow (p. 99)

Lemon Mousse (p. 108)
or
Apple and Pineapple Crumble (p. 54)

3.
Grapefruit or citrus *compote*
or
Cool Cucumber Soup (p. 71)

Savoury Vegetable Curry (p. 192)
and
Sweet Spicy Curry (p. 144)
Almond and Pepper Rice (p. 131)
and
Plain brown rice
Assorted salads and sambals (p. 142)

Tropical Fruit Salad (p. 154)
Lemon Sorbet (p. 203)

4.
Mushroom Pancakes in Tomato Sauce (p. 140)

Cheese and Olive Flan (p. 135) with fresh tomatoes
Green Pea and Spring Bean Salads (pp. 83 and 31)

Port Wine Apples (p. 153) with cream
or
Almond-topped Apples (p. 53)

5.
Individual servings of Watercress and Citrus
Fruit Salad (p. 86)

Vegetable Soufflé (summer p. 102 or winter p. 195)
French Beans and New Potatoes in Lemon Chive Sauce (p. 89))

Spicy Apple or Banana Pudding (p. 154)
Cottage Cheese Tortoni (p. 57)

6.
Stuffed Peppers with Eggs (p. 100)

Brazil Nut and Tomato Loaf (p. 134)
and/or
Carrot and Nut Loaf (p. 177)
Courgette Casserole (p. 93)

Caramelled Fresh Fruit (p. 147) with cream or yogurt (p. 112)
Ice Cream (p. 110)
with
Orange and Lemon Sauce (p. 153)

7.
Avocado and Mushroom Entrée (p. 122)

Cauliflower and Tomato Crumble with Hazelnuts (p. 91)
Green salad

Fresh Fruit Mousse (p. 108)
or
Raspberry Jelly (p. 205)

8.
Egg Mayonnaise Roll (p. 24)
with
Salad and Hot Breads (p. 214)

Almond-stuffed Marrow (p. 132)
or
Savoury Stuffed Marrow (p. 143)
Steamed carrots and fresh beans

Brandied Apricots (p. 199)
Exotic Fruit salad (p. 106) with cream

9.
Gingered Bean Sprouts and Mushrooms (p. 124)
or
Cream of Asparagus Soup (p. 72)

Rich Walnut Savoury (p. 189)
Fresh butter beans tossed in French dressing (p. 171)

Apple Snow (p. 104)
or
Apple Cake (p. 103)

10.
Individual servings of Sweet Corn Casserole (p. 143)
or
Gazpacho (p. 73)

Baked Omelette (p. 36)
Baked Stuffed Potatoes (p. 133)
Fresh steamed beans

Cottage Cheese and Peaches (p. 105)
Cantaloupe and Passion Fruit Salad (p. 201)

11.
Individual servings of Cucumber and Pineapple Salad (p. 82)
or
Asparagus Pancakes (p. 21)

Courgettes Au Gratin (p. 87)
or
Spinach Tagliatelle in Tomato Sauce (p. 193)
Green Salad Galore (p. 83)

Cheesecake (p. 56)
Honeydew Spicy Salad (p. 59)

12.
Individual servings of Ratatouille (p. 98) sprinkled with fresh parsley
or
Spinach Cream Soup (p. 24)

Cauliflower and Noodle Bake (p. 91)
or
Leeks and Pasta in Tomato Sauce (p. 42)
Green salad

Baked Apples (p. 198) with cream or yogurt (p. 112)
Green and Gold Fruit salad (p. 58)

13.
Asparagus Pancakes (p. 21)
or
Baked Eggs (p. 21)

Cottage Cheese and Oat Loaf (p. 137)
Steamed carrots and courgettes
Tomato and Onion Pie (p. 101)

Fresh Fruit Salad (p. 106)
Dried Fruit in Wine with cream (p. 57)

14.
Individual servings of Eggs Florentine (p. 40)

Lentil Hot Pot (p. 178)

Ice Cream (p. 110) with fresh fruit
or
Grape Fruit Salad (p. 58)

15.
Savoury Pots of Cheese (p. 76) with *crudités* (p. 124)

Lentil Pancakes with Parsley Sauce (p. 44)

Apple and Mint Salad (p. 53)
or
Rhubarb Fool (p. 61)

16.
Eggs and Cheese on Toast (p. 166)
Carrot and Apple and Green Pea Salads (pp. 127 and 83)

Individual servings of Potato Pie (p. 187) with various fillings, garnished with tomatoes
or
Lasagne (p. 138)
Green salad

Fresh fruit with yogurt (p. 112) garnished with toasted sesame seeds

17.
Individual servings of Cabbage and Tomatoes (p. 135)

Slow Omelette (p. 50) garnished with sliced mushrooms,
sunflower seeds and grated cheese
Green Salad Galore (p. 83)

Avocado and Lime Delight (p. 55)
or
Fresh fruit with Sunshine Biscuits (p. 216)
Apricot Almond Delight (p. 197)
or
Date and Cashew Rounds (p. 202)

18.
Individual Vegetable Soufflés (p. 102)

Savoury Stuffed Marrow (p. 143)
Steamed carrots and greens
Roast parsnips and gravy

Cottage Cheese Tortoni (p. 57)
Apple and Pear Fruit Salad (p. 147)

19.
Individual servings of Butter Beans Au Gratin (p. 90)
or
Tomato and Onion Pancakes (p. 25)

Seasonal Vegetables in Savoury Sauce (p. 49)
Green salad

Cottage Cheese with Pineapple and Mint (p. 105)
or
Banana and Apple Zesty Salad (p. 55)

20.
Thick slices of marrow with Almond and Onion Loaf stuffing (p. 33)
garnished with tomato slices and grated cheese

Spinach Pancakes in Cheese Sauce (p. 51)

Fresh Fruit Salad (p. 106) with cream or Ice Cream (p. 110)
or
Fruit Shortcake (p. 58)

Festive Breakfasts

1.

Pikelets (p. 60) served in a lined basket with
Home-made Jams (p. 108)
Marmalade (p. 152)
Orange and Lemon Sauce (p. 153)
Butter and honey with lemon wedges and tahini
Sunflower seed spread with honey or yeast extract
Peanut butter
Raw cane sugar and cinnamon

2.

Puffed Deloons (p. 111)
served with butter and lemon wedges

3.

Assorted hot bread rolls (p. 212) topped with seeds or cracked wheat
Serve with butter, yeast extract, boiled eggs, bel paese or Swiss cheese

4.

Pancakes (p. 141) served with
Cottage Cheese and Almonds (p. 148)
Cottage Cheese and Walnuts (p. 202)
Cottage Cheese and Apple (p. 56)
Boiled egg, chopped and moistened with cream, flavoured with fresh herbs
Sautéed tomatoes, onions and sweet basil
Cottage cheese, sieved and mixed with herbs or yeast extract
Poached egg sprinkled with black pepper and sea salt

Serve the pancakes either separately, with the fillings in bowls, or ready-filled on platters.

5.
Silesian Pancakes (p. 62)
served with butter, honey and lemon juice

6.
Fresh Fruit Salads (p. 106) with muesli
Prof. Shears' Muesli (p. 110)—very nutritious
Nut and Seed Muesli (p. 59)—lower in carbohydrate
Sweet Toasted Oat Snack (p. 112)—more easily absorbed than raw muesli

Arrange all the mueslis and fruit salads in individual bowls and serve with jugs of fruit juice, milk and cream

7.
Home-made yogurt (p. 112) served with fresh or stewed fruit
or a *compote* of soaked dried fruit

Serve the yogurt in a large glass dish surrounded by smaller dishes of sliced bananas, apples, pears and citrus fruits, with bunches of grapes between them. The *compote* of dried fruits and the single stewed fruit may be sprinkled with wheat germ or bran.

8.
Baked Apples (p. 198)
Jugs of yogurt (p. 112), cream and buttermilk

9.
Egg Nog (p. 150)
Home-made bread or rolls (pp. 211 and 212)
Home-made jam (p. 108) or marmalade (p. 152)
Fresh fruit

10.
Fresh fruit juice
Poached eggs on wholemeal toast with grilled tomatoes and mushrooms,
garnished with sprigs of watercress or parsley

11.
Italian Summer Breakfast
Hot wholemeal toast rubbed with garlic, sprinkled with olive oil, fresh rosemary and sweet basil or black pepper. Cut into thick fingers and serve immediately, accompanied by a large bowl of ripe tomatoes, cut into slices or wedges. Pile the tomatoes onto the toast and eat with the fingers.

Special Occasion Menus

CHRISTMAS EVE SUPPER

Savoury Pots of Cheese (p. 76)
Avocado Cream with Mushrooms (p. 163)
Crudités (p. 124)

Vegetable Risotto (p. 194)
Mushroom and Cashew Nut Flan (p. 183)
Green Salad Galore (p. 83)

Lychees and Melon Fruit Salad (p. 204)
or
Cantaloupe and Passion Fruit Salad (p. 201)

A dessert course of nuts and dried fruit,
fresh fruit and Apricot Almond Delight (p. 197)

CHRISTMAS DAY DINNER

Gazpacho (p. 73)
or
Celery and Mushroom Entrée (p. 123)

Walnut Loaf with Orange Sauce (p. 146)
Tomato and Onion Pie (p. 101)
Steamed Brussels sprouts and carrots
Roast potatoes and parsnips

Wine Fruit Mince (p. 209)
Ice Cream (p. 110)
or
Rich or Light Christmas Pudding (pp. 206 and 204)
with
Brandy Butter (p. 200)
or
White Sauce (p. 208)
Lemon Sorbet (p. 203)
or
Raspberry Jelly (p. 205)

Cheese Board

BOXING DAY LUNCH

Glazed Carrots and Asparagus (p. 74)

Cheese Flan (p. 92) with leeks
Topped Tomatoes (p. 26)
Green Platter (p. 83)
Cucumber and Apple Salad (p. 82)

Apple Snow (p. 104)
Brandied Apricots (p. 199)
Exotic Fruit Salad (p. 106)
Ice Cream (p. 110)

NEW YEAR'S EVE BUFFET

Jacket baked potatoes
Peanut Bake (p. 45)
Almond and Onion Loaf (p. 33)
Brazil Nut and Tomato Loaf (p. 134)
Savoury Pots of Cheese (p. 76)
Stuffed Eggs (p. 80)
Egg Mayonnaise Roll (p. 24)

Bean Sprouts and Rice Salad (p. 171)
Haricot Salad (p. 29)
Green Salad Galore (p. 83)
Carrot and Apple Salad (p. 127)
Red Cabbage Salad (p. 173)

An old-fashioned dessert course:
Cheese board and biscuits
Bowls of shelled and unshelled nuts
Fresh fruit
Platters of dried fruit
Australian Christmas Cake (p. 198)

NEW YEAR'S DAY LUNCHEON

Avocado and Tomato Entrée (p. 71)

Lasagne (p. 138)
Green Salad Galore (p. 83)

Chocolate Mousse (p. 148)
Fresh Fruit Salad (p. 106)

EASTER SUNDAY DINNER

Eggs Florentine (p. 40)

Brazil Nut and Tomato Loaf (p. 134)
Broccoli, new potatoes and young carrots

Chocolate Mousse (p. 148)
or
Port Wine Apples (p. 153)
Apple and Mint Salad (p. 53)

SUMMER SUNDAY LUNCH
or
SUPPER PARTY

To be Served Outside

Grapefruit and orange *compote*
French beans in tomato dressing (p. 86)

Pizza (p. 184)
Courgettes Au Gratin (p. 87)
Cheese and Onion Flan (p. 92)
Green Platter (p. 83)
Hot and Cold Salad (p. 84)
Cucumber and Apple Salad (p. 82)
Green and Red Salad (p. 82)
Tomato and Mint Salad (p. 85)
Sprout and One Salad (p. 173)

Raspberry Mousse (p. 108)
Avocado and Lime Delight (p. 55)
Strawberries or peaches
with
Fresh or soured cream
Tropical Fruit Salad (p. 154)

FIFTH OF NOVEMBER CELEBRATIONS

A Supper After the Bonfire and Fireworks

Autumn Glory Soup (p. 122)
Autumn Minestrone Soup (p. 121)
Mushroom Soup (p. 126)
Cream of Onion Soup (p. 123)
(served in wide mugs)

Sweet corn on the cob
Baked Stuffed Potatoes (p. 133)
Cauliflower and Tomato Crumble with Hazelnuts (p. 91)
Aubergine and Pepper Pasta (p. 88)
Bean Sprouts and Rice Salad (p. 171)
Green Salad Galore (p. 83)
Cole-slaw (p. 128)

Gingerbread Men (p. 213)
Sunshine Biscuits (p. 216)
Oatmeal Molasses Biscuits (p. 215)

Apples and Nuts

For Those on Restricted Diets

Main Courses Without Dairy Products

Peanut Bake (p. 45)
Lentil Roast (p. 179)
Lentil Hot Pot (p. 178)
Spinach and Buckwheat Bake (p. 51)
(Use well flavoured stock and vegetable oil to make the white sauce.)
Cabbage and Tomatoes (p. 135)
Courgette Casserole (p. 93)
Savoury Vegetable Curry (p. 192)
Sweet Spicy Curry (p. 144)
Almond and Pepper Rice (p. 131)
Ratatouille (p. 98)
Gingered Bean Sprouts and Mushrooms (p. 124)
Seasonal Vegetables in Savoury Sauce (p. 49)
Some Baked Stuffed Potatoes (p. 133)
Wholemeal pasta and savoury vegetable sauces, sprinkled with parsley or nuts. In the
recipe for Lasagne (p. 138), use only well flavoured stock and vegetable oil to make the
sauce.
Some tvp dishes
Some bean dishes
Hearty soups make a meal with a salad

Main Courses with Eggs but No Other Dairy Products

Eggs Florentine (p. 40)
(Use well flavoured stock and vegetable oil to make the white sauce.)
Pancake Omelette (p. 140)
Most loaf recipes

Main Courses Without Gluten-containing Grains
(Wheat, oats, barley and buckwheat)

Omit all loaves, pasta dishes, quiches and pies.
Concentrate on vegetable casseroles, some egg and cheese dishes, substituting rice and corn flours for wheat.

Low-fat Diet
(Use only cold-pressed vegetable oils, sparingly)

Concentrate on vegetable casseroles, curries, salads and soups. Add 'body' to casseroles and soups with wheat germ and bran.
Thicken sauces etc. by making a paste of wholemeal flour and cold vegetable stock or water, and then gradually add the rest of the liquid hot, whisking vigorously over a low heat.
Avoid cheese (except cottage cheese) and eggs (eat only 1-2 eggs per week).

Index